MW01629866

AS·NON·FLECTES
PEU

16 knitting designs in
Cashmere Tweed & Wool
Tweed by Martin Storey

The romantic grounds and majestic rooms of Dunrobin castle in Scotland are the perfect backdrop for a collection of sumptuous and soft tweed knits designed for the stylish laird and his lady. Classic Tweed is a versatile collection introducing two new yarns to the Rowan Classic range, which really are the height of luxury. Classic Cashmere Tweed and Classic Wool Tweed come in a rich palette inspired by the colour blends in Scottish textiles from classic tweed weaves to traditional tartans. In their natural location, the garments allow the quality of the yarns to really shine out. Ribbed sweaters, scoop necks, shrugs and easy to knit accessories are a delight.

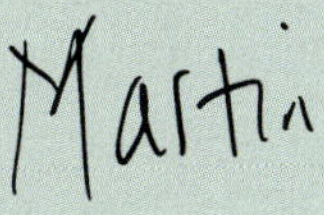

the designs

Sumptuous and soft tweed knits in luxurious yarns
bring a tale of romance in the Highlands alive.

16 **Fenella** ▲
Cashmere Tweed or
Wool Tweed
Pattern page 42

18 **Logan** ▲
Cashmere Tweed or
Wool Tweed
Pattern page 43

20 **Glen hat, scarf & mitts** ✚
Cashmere Tweed or
Wool Tweed
Pattern page 47 & 48

22 **Edina** ▲
Cashmere Tweed or
Wool Tweed
Pattern page 40

32 **Ross** [mens version] ★
Cashmere Tweed or
Wool Tweed
Pattern page 53

33 **Moira** ▲
Cashmere Tweed or
Wool Tweed
Pattern page 59

34 **Minna** ▲
Cashmere Tweed or
Wool Tweed
Pattern page 57

SIZE KEY: ● Size 8 - 22 ▲ Size S - XL ★ Size S - XXL (Mens) ✚ Accessory (Refer to pattern page)

tweed
ross [woman]
george
lewis [woman]
lewis [man]
montrose
ross [man]
fenella
nessa
glen hat [man]
moira
minna
logan

designersnotebook

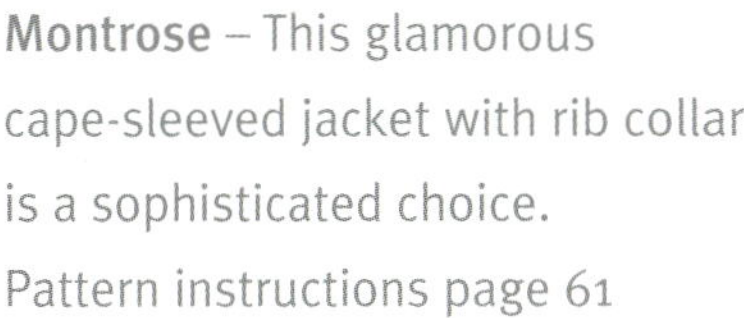

Montrose – This glamorous
cape-sleeved jacket with rib collar
is a sophisticated choice.
Pattern instructions page 61

Mac – A rugged polo collar sweater in a wide
rib stitch to create a wonderful texture
Pattern instructions page 55

Lewis – A semi-fitted, luxurious
crew-neck sweater with flattering
raglan sleeves in a garter stitch.
Pattern instructions page 51

Ross [Mens version] – With wide stripes and raglan sleeves this fashionable v-neck sweater is easy to knit. Pattern instructions page 67

Fenella – Our oversized sleeveless tunic has deep armholes and a wonderfully soft cowl collar. Pattern instructions page 42

Logan – A delightful shrug with a sophisticated slash wide neck in a moss rib stitch. Pattern instructions page 43

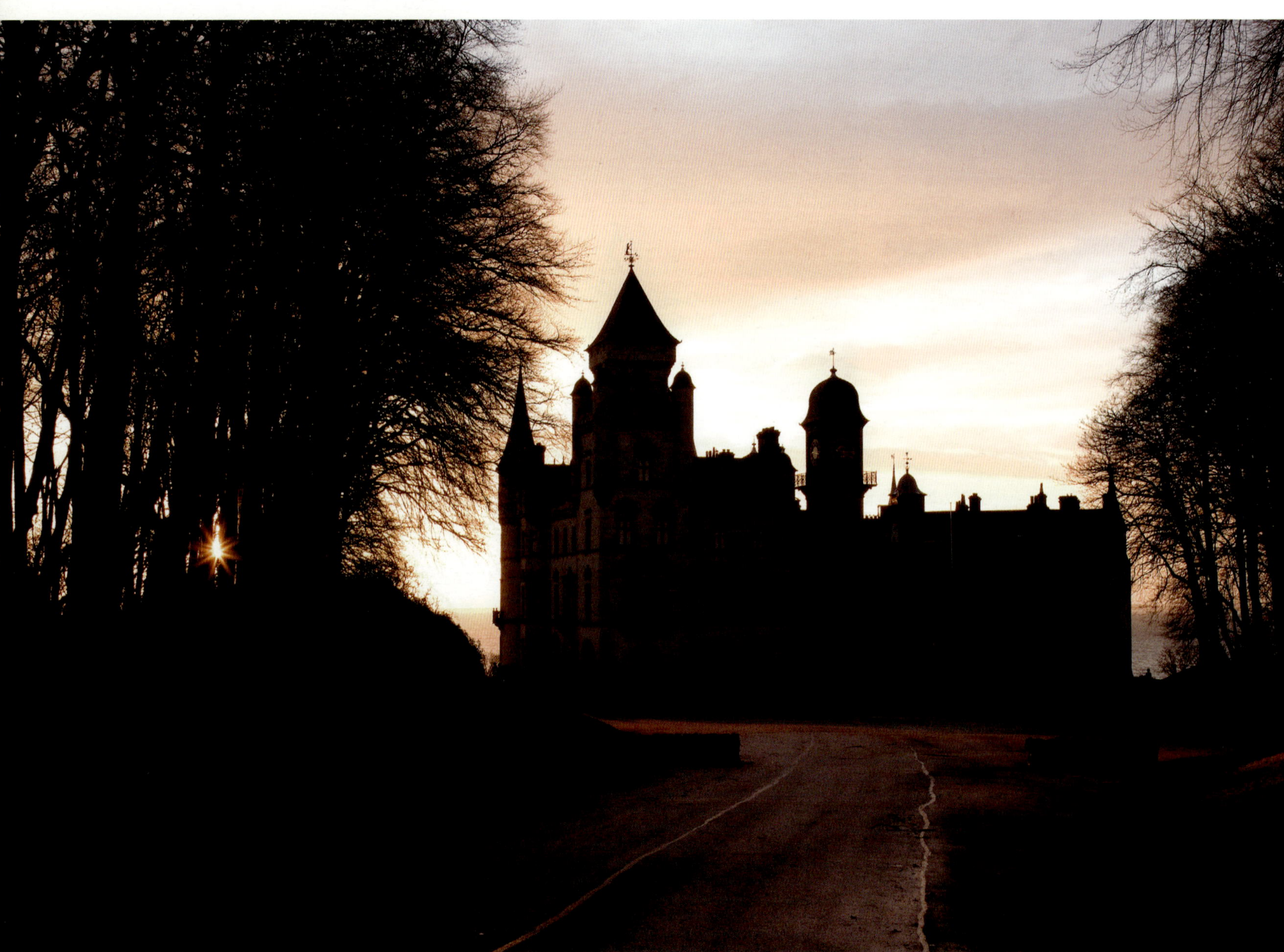

Glen Man hat, scarf & mitts for him and her – A wonderful gift for
the man in your life, this very simple rib makes our hat, scarf and
mitts [mens version only] perfect for a cold winter's day. The yarn
is so luxurious and cosy that you will want to knit yourself a set
as well. Pattern instructions page 47 & 48

Edina – This scoop neck sweater is elegant enough for a castle with its cabled belt detail and a flattering, deep cable and rib hem. Pattern instructions page 40

Glen scarf – A simple rib scarf. Pattern instructions page 48

Ross [ladies version] – Our wide stripe v-neck sweater
is semi-fitted with raglan sleeves for an elegant shape.
Pattern instructions page 65

Elegant surroundings conjure up a romantic history and so time passes

Iona – A fashionable plunge v-neck sweater with a drawstring hem. Pattern instructions page 49

George – This men's jacket is decorated with a wonderful rope cable with rib collar. Pattern instructions page 44

Tapestry colours, warm knits take us from day to evening.
Keep the cold of winter at bay.

AS·NON·FLECTES·
PEUR

Nessa – an intriguingly cabled sweater with a deep shaped rollover collar. Pattern instructions page 63

Lewis [Mens version]
A classic crew neck
sweater in a garter stitch
with raglan sleeves.
Pattern instructions
page 53

Moira – Our wonderful
sleeveless shrug is
flatteringly shaped and
the wide rib collar looks
great fastened with a pin
or brooch
Pattern instructions
page 59

Minna – The picture of elegance, this shawl collar wrap cardigan ties with a pretty ribbon
Pattern instructions page 57

Tension

Obtaining the correct tension is perhaps the single factor which can make the difference between a successful garment and a disastrous one. It controls both the shape and size of an article, so any variation, however slight, can distort the finished garment. Different designers feature in our books and it is **their** tension, given at the **start** of each pattern, which you must match. We recommend that you knit a square in pattern and/or stocking stitch (depending on the pattern instructions) of perhaps 5 - 10 more stitches and 5 - 10 more rows than those given in the tension note. Mark out the central 10cm square with pins. If you have too many stitches to 10cm try again using thicker needles, if you have too few stitches to 10cm try again using finer needles. Once you have achieved the correct tension your garment will be knitted to the measurements indicated in the size diagram shown at the end of the pattern.

Sizing and Size Diagram Note

The instructions are given for the smallest size. Where they vary, work the figures in brackets for the larger sizes. **One set of figures refers to all sizes.** Included with most patterns in this magazine is a **'size diagram'**, or sketch of the finished garment and its dimensions. The size diagram shows the finished width of the garment at the under-arm point, and it is this measurement that the knitter should choose first; a useful tip is to measure one of your own garments which is a comfortable fit. Having chosen a size based on width, look at the corresponding length for that size; if you are not happy with the total length which we recommend, adjust your own garment before beginning your armhole shaping - any adjustment after this point will mean that your sleeve will not fit into your garment easily - don't forget to take your adjustment into account if there is any side seam shaping. Finally, look at the sleeve length; the size diagram shows the finished sleeve measurement, taking into account any top-arm insertion length. Measure your body between the centre of your neck and your wrist, this measurement should correspond to half the garment width plus the sleeve length. Again, your sleeve length may be adjusted, but remember to take into consideration your sleeve increases if you do adjust the length - you must increase more frequently than the pattern states to shorten your sleeve, less frequently to lengthen it.

Chart Note

Many of the patterns in the book are worked from charts. Each square on a chart represents a stitch and each line of squares a row of knitting. Each colour used is given a different letter and these are shown in the **materials** section, or in the **key** alongside the chart of each pattern. When working from the charts, read odd rows (K) from right to left and even rows (P) from left to right, unless otherwise stated.

Knitting with colour

There are two main methods of working colour into a knitted fabric: Intarsia and Fairisle techniques. The first method produces a single thickness of fabric and is usually used where a colour is only required in a particular area of a row and does not form a repeating pattern across the row, as in the fairisle technique.

Intarsia: The simplest way to do this is to cut short lengths of yarn for each motif or block of colour used in a row. Then joining in the various colours at the appropriate point on the row, link one colour to the next by twisting them around each other where they meet on the wrong side to avoid gaps. All ends can then either be darned along the colour join lines, as each motif is completed or then can be "knitted-in" to the fabric of the knitting as each colour is worked into the pattern. This is done in much the same way as "weaving-in" yarns when working the Fairisle technique and does save time darning-in ends. It is essential that the tension is noted for Intarsia as this may vary from the stocking stitch if both are used in the same pattern.

Fairisle type knitting: When two or three colours are worked repeatedly across a row, strand the yarn not in use loosely behind the stitches being worked. If you are working with more than two colours, treat the "floating"yarns as if they were one yarn and always spread the stitches to their correct width to keep them elastic. It is advisable not to carry the stranded or "floating" yarns over more than three stitches at a time, but to weave them under and over the colour you are working. The "floating" yarns are caught at the back of the work.

Finishing Instructions

After working for hours knitting a garment, it seems a great pity that many garments are spoiled because such little care is taken in the pressing and finishing process. Follow the following tips for a truly professional-looking garment.

Pressing

Block out each piece of knitting and following the instructions on the ball band press the garment pieces, omitting the ribs. Tip: Take special care to press the edges, as this will make sewing up both easier and neater. If the ball band indicates that the fabric is not to be pressed, then covering the blocked out fabric with a damp white cotton cloth and leaving it to stand will have the desired effect. Darn in all ends neatly along the selvedge edge or a colour join, as appropriate.

Stitching

When stitching the pieces together, remember to match areas of colour and texture very carefully where they meet. Use a seam stitch such as back stitch or mattress stitch for all main knitting seams and join all ribs and neckband with mattress stitch, unless otherwise stated.

Construction

Having completed the pattern instructions, join left shoulder and neckband seams as detailed above. Sew the top of the sleeve to the body of the garment using the method detailed in the pattern, referring to the appropriate guide:

Set-in sleeves: Place centre of cast-off edge of sleeve to shoulder seam. Set in sleeve, easing sleeve head into armhole.

Straight cast-off sleeves: Place centre of cast-off edge of sleeve to shoulder seam. Sew top of sleeve to body.

Join side and sleeve seams.
Slip stitch pocket edgings and linings into place. Sew on buttons to correspond with buttonholes. Ribbed welts and neckbands and any area of garter stitch should not be pressed.

Abbreviations

K	knit	psso	pass slipped
P	purl		stitch over
st(s)	stitch(es)	tbl	through back
inc	increas(e)(ing)		of loop
dec	decreas(e)(ing)	M1	make one stitch
st st	stocking stitch		by picking up
	(1 row K, 1 row P)		horizontal loop
g st	garter stitch		before next stitch
	(K every row)		and working into
beg	begin(ning)		back of it
foll	following	yrn	yarn round needle
rem	remain(ing)	yfwd	yarn forward
rep	repeat	yon	yarn over needle
alt	alternate	yfrn	yarn forward and
cont	continue		round needle
patt	pattern	meas	measures
tog	together	0	no stitches,
mm	millimetres		times, or rows
cm	centimetres	-	no stitches, times
in(s)	inch(es)		or rows for that
RS	right side		size
WS	wrong side	approx	approximately
sl 1	slip one stitch	rev	reverse
sl 2	slip two stitches		

Main image page 22

Edina

YARN

	8	10	12	14	16	18	
To fit bust	81	86	91	97	102	107	cm
	32	34	36	38	40	42	in

Rowan RYC Cashmere Tweed

	17	17	18	19	20	21	x 25gm

(photographed in Sisal 852)

Rowan RYC Wool Tweed

	9	9	9	10	10	11	x 50gm

NEEDLES

Cashmere Tweed version
1 pair 5mm (no 6) (US 8) needles
1 pair 6mm (no 4) (US 10) needles
5mm (no 6) (US 8) circular needle
Cable needle

Wool Tweed version
1 pair 4½mm (no 7) (US 7) needles
1 pair 5½mm (no 5) (US 9) needles
1 pair 4½mm (no 7) (US 7) circular needle
Cable needle

EXTRAS – 7 cm buckle (ref 00367). 90 [95: 100: 105: 110: 115] cm of 5 cm wide petersham ribbon.

TENSION

18 sts and 24 rows to 10 cm measured over stocking stitch using larger size needles.

SPECIAL ABBREVIATIONS

C6B = slip next 3 sts onto cable needle and leave at back of work, K3, then K3 from cable needle;
C6F = slip next 3 sts onto cable needle and leave at front of work, K3, then K3 from cable needle.

BACK

Using smaller needles cast on 78 [82: 86: 92: 96: 102] sts.
Row 1 (RS): K0 [0: 0: 1: 0: 0], P0 [2: 0: 2: 1: 0], *K2, P2, rep from * to last 2 [0: 2: 1: 3: 2] sts, K2 [0: 2: 1: 2: 2], P0 [0: 0: 0: 1: 0].
Row 2: P0 [0: 0: 1: 0: 0], K0 [2: 0: 2: 1: 0], *P2, K2, rep from * to last 2 [0: 2: 1: 3: 2] sts, P2 [0: 2: 1: 2: 2], K0 [0: 0: 0: 1: 0].

These 2 rows form rib.
Work in rib for 1 row more.
Row 4 (WS): Rib 16 [18: 20: 23: 25: 28], (M1, rib 1) 3 times, (rib 1, M1) 3 times, rib 34, (M1, rib 1) 3 times, (rib 1, M1) 3 times, rib to end.
90 [94: 98: 104: 108: 114] sts.
Change to larger needles.
Row 5: Rib 14 [16: 18: 21: 23: 26], K16, rib 30, K16, rib to end.
Row 6: Rib 14 [16: 18: 21: 23: 26], K2, P12, K2, rib 30, K2, P12, K2, rib to end.
Row 7: Rib 14 [16: 18: 21: 23: 26], K2, C6B, C6F, K2, rib 30, K2, C6B, C6F, K2, rib to end.
Row 8: As row 6.
Rows 9 to 12: As rows 5 and 6, twice.
Rows 5 to 12 form cable patt.
Cont in cable patt for a further 26 rows, ending with RS facing for next row.
Make belt slots
Row 39 (RS): Rib 14 [16: 18: 21: 23: 26], slip next 16 sts onto a holder and, in their place, turn and cast on 10 sts, turn, rib 30, slip next 16 sts onto 2nd holder and, in their place, turn and cast on 10 sts, turn, rib to end.
78 [82: 86: 92: 96: 102] sts.
Work in rib (as set by rows 1 and 2) across all sts for 14 rows, ending with **WS** facing for next row.
Row 54 (WS): Rib 14 [16: 18: 21: 23: 26], cast off next 10 sts, rib until there are 30 sts on right needle after cast-off, cast off next 10 sts, rib to end.
Break yarn and leave sts on 3rd holder.
With RS facing, rejoin yarn to one set of 16 sts left on a holder, patt to end.
Work a further 15 rows in patt on these 16 sts only, ending with RS facing for next row.
Break yarn and leave sts on another holder.
With RS facing, rejoin yarn to other set of 16 sts left on a holder, patt to end.
Work a further 15 rows in patt on these 16 sts only, ending with RS facing for next row.
Break yarn and leave sts on another holder.
Join sections
With RS facing, rejoin yarn and cont as folls:
Row 55 (RS): Rib first 14 [16: 18: 21: 23: 26] sts of main section left on 3rd holder, patt next 16 sts of first patt strip, rib next 30 sts of main section left on 3rd holder, patt next 16 sts of other patt strip, rib rem 14 [16: 18: 21: 23: 26] sts of main section left on 3rd holder. 90 [94: 98: 104: 108: 114] sts.
Row 56: Patt 16 [18: 20: 23: 25: 28] sts, (P2tog) 6 times, patt 34 sts, (P2tog) 6 times, patt to end.
78 [82: 86: 92: 96: 102] sts.
Beg with a K row, work in st st until back meas 38 [38: 37: 40: 39: 41] cm, ending with RS facing for next row.
Shape armholes
Cast off 4 [5: 5: 6: 6: 7] sts at beg of next 2 rows.
70 [72: 76: 80: 84: 88] sts.**
Dec 1 st at each end of next 3 [3: 5: 5: 5: 5] rows, then on foll 2 [2: 1: 2: 2: 3] alt rows, then on foll 4th row. 58 [60: 62: 64: 68: 70] sts.
Cont straight until armhole meas 20 [20: 21: 21: 22: 22] cm, ending with RS facing for next row.
Shape shoulders and back neck
Cast off 4 [4: 5: 5: 5: 6] sts at beg of next 2 rows.
50 [52: 52: 54: 58: 58] sts.
Next row (RS): Cast off 4 [4: 5: 5: 5: 6] sts, K until there are 8 [9: 8: 9: 10: 9] sts on right needle and turn, leaving rem sts on a holder.
Work each side of neck separately.
Cast off 4 sts at beg of next row.
Cast off rem 4 [5: 4: 5: 6: 5] sts.
With RS facing, rejoin yarn to rem sts, cast off centre 26 [26: 26: 26: 28: 28] sts, K to end.
Complete to match first side, reversing shapings.

FRONT

Work as given for back to **.
Dec 1 st at each end of next 3 [3: 5: 4: 5: 5] rows.
64 [66: 66: 72: 74: 78] sts.
Work 1 [1: 1: 0: 1: 1] row, ending with RS facing for next row.
Shape neck
Next row (RS): K2tog, K24 [25: 25: 29: 29: 31] and turn, leaving rem sts on a holder.
Work each side of neck separately.
Dec 1 st at neck edge of next 6 rows, then on foll 1 [1: 1: 2: 2: 2] alt rows, then on 2 foll 4th rows, then on 2 foll 6th rows **and at same time** dec 1 st at armhole edge of 2nd [2nd: 4th: 2nd: 2nd: 2nd] and foll 0 [0: 0: 1: 0: 1] alt rows, then on 1 [1: 0: 1: 1: 1] foll 4th row. 12 [13: 14: 15: 16: 17] sts.

Cont straight until front matches back to beg of
shoulder shaping, ending with RS facing for next
row.

Shape shoulder

Cast off 4 [4: 5: 5: 5: 6] sts at beg of next and foll
alt row.

Work 1 row.

Cast off rem 4 [5: 4: 5: 6: 5] sts.

With RS facing, rejoin yarn to rem sts, cast off
centre 12 [12: 12: 10: 12: 12] sts, K to last 2 sts,
K2tog.

Complete to match first side, reversing shapings.

SLEEVES

Using smaller needles cast on 42 [42: 42: 42:
46: 46] sts.

Row 1 (RS): K2, *P2, K2, rep from * to end.

Row 2: P2, *K2, P2, rep from * to end.

These 2 rows form rib.

Work in rib for a further 20 rows, inc 0 [0: 1: 1:
0: 0] st at each end of last row and ending with
RS facing for next row. 42 [42: 44: 44: 46: 46] sts.
Change to larger needles.

Beg with a K row, work in st st, shaping sides by
inc 1 st at each end of 7th [7th: 7th: 7th: 7th: 5th]
and every foll 8th [8th: 8th: 8th: 8th: 6th] row to
46 [56: 54: 64: 64: 52] sts, then on every foll
10th [10th: 10th: -: 10th: 8th] row until there are
58 [60: 62: -: 66: 68] sts.

Cont straight until sleeve meas 45 [45: 46: 46:
47: 47] cm, ending with RS facing for next row.

Shape top

Cast off 4 [5: 5: 6: 6: 7] sts at beg of next 2 rows.
50 [50: 52: 52: 54: 54] sts.

Dec 1 st at each end of next 3 rows, then on foll
3 alt rows, then on every foll 4th row until 30 [30:
32: 32: 34: 34] sts rem.

Work 1 row, ending with RS facing for next row.

Dec 1 st at each end of next and every foll alt row
to 24 sts, then on foll 3 rows, ending with RS

facing for next row.
Cast off rem 18 sts.

MAKING UP

Press as described on the information page.
Join both shoulder seams using back stitch, or
mattress stitch if preferred.

Neckband

With RS facing and using circular needle, beg and
ending at left shoulder seam, pick up and knit 46
[46: 46: 47: 47: 49] sts down left side of neck, 12
[12: 12: 10: 12: 12] sts from front, 46 [46: 46: 47:
47: 49] sts up right side of neck, then 28 [28: 28:
28: 30: 30] sts from back. 132 [132: 132: 132: 136:
140] sts.

Round 1 (RS): *K2, P2, rep from * to end.
Rep last round 7 times more.
Cast off in rib.

Belt

Using 5mm (US 8) needles cast on 16 sts.

Row 1 (RS): K16.

Row 2: K2, P12, K2.

Row 3: K2, C6B, C6F, K2.

Row 4: As row 2.

Rows 5 to 8: As rows 1 and 2, twice.

These 8 rows form patt.

Cont in patt until belt meas 86 [91: 96: 101:
106: 111] cm, ending with RS facing for next row.
Cast off.

See information page for finishing instructions,
setting in sleeves using the set-in method. Lay
petersham ribbon onto WS of belt, turn under
raw ends and slip stitch in place. Thread one end
of belt onto buckle and secure in place. Thread
belt through belt slots as in photograph and
fasten at centre front.

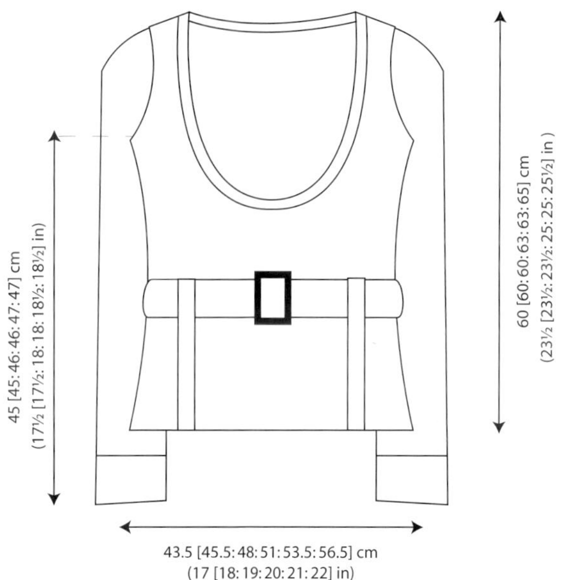

Main image page 16

 **Fenella**

YARN

	S	M	L	XL	
To fit bust	81-86	91-97	102-107	112-117	cm
	32-34	36-38	40-42	44-46	in

Rowan RYC Cashmere Tweed

	35	39	44	47	x 25gm

Rowan RYC Wool Tweed

	18	20	22	24	x 50gm

(photographed in Shetland 953)

NEEDLES

Cashmere Tweed version
1 pair 5mm (no 6) (US 8) needles
1 pair 6mm (no 4) (US 10) needles
5mm (no 6) (US 8) circular needle
6mm (no 4) (US 10) circular needle

Wool Tweed version
1 pair 4½mm (no 7) (US 7) needles
1 pair 5½mm (no 5) (US 9) needles
1 pair 4½mm (no 7) (US 7) circular needle
1 pair 5½mm (no 5) (US 9) circular needle

TENSION

18 sts and 24 rows to 10 cm measured over stocking stitch using larger size needles.

BACK

Using smaller needles cast on 86 [98: 106: 118] sts.
Row 1 (RS): P2, *K2, P2, rep from * to end.
Row 2: K2, *P2, K2, rep from * to end.
These 2 rows form rib.
Work in rib for a further 70 rows, inc 1 [0: 1: 0] st at each end of last row and ending with RS facing for next row. 88 [98: 108: 118] sts.
Change to larger needles.
Beg with a K row, work in st st until back meas 32 [33: 34: 35] cm, ending with RS facing for next row.
Shape for sleeves
Inc 1 st at each end of next and foll 3 alt rows, then on foll 3 rows, ending with RS facing for next row. 102 [112: 122: 132] sts.

Cast on 4 sts at beg of next 2 rows, then 5 sts at beg of foll 2 rows, then 10 sts at beg of next 2 rows. 140 [150: 160: 170] sts.
Cont straight until armhole meas 33 [34: 35: 36] cm from last set of cast-on sts, ending with RS facing for next row.
Shape shoulders and back neck
Cast off 18 [20: 21: 23] sts at beg of next 2 rows. 104 [110: 118: 124] sts.
Next row (RS): Cast off 18 [20: 21: 23] sts, K until there are 22 [23: 25: 26] sts on right needle and turn, leaving rem sts on a holder.
Work each side of neck separately.
Cast off 4 sts at beg of next row.
Cast off rem 18 [19: 21: 22] sts.
With RS facing, rejoin yarn to rem sts, cast off centre 24 [24: 26: 26] sts, K to end.
Complete to match first side, reversing shapings.

FRONT

Work as given for back until 32 [32: 34: 34] rows less have been worked than on back to beg of shoulder shaping, ending with RS facing for next row.
Shape neck
Next row (RS): K64 [69: 74: 79] and turn, leaving rem sts on a holder.
Work each side of neck separately.
Dec 1 st at neck edge of next 4 rows, then on foll 2 [2: 3: 3] alt rows, then on 4 foll 4th rows. 54 [59: 63: 68] sts.
Work 7 rows, ending with RS facing for next row.
Shape shoulder
Cast off 18 [20: 21: 23] sts at beg of next and foll alt row.
Work 1 row.
Cast off rem 18 [19: 21: 22] sts.
With RS facing, rejoin yarn to rem sts, cast off centre 12 sts, K to end.
Complete to match first side, reversing shapings.

MAKING UP

Press as described on the information page.
Join both shoulder seams using back stitch, or mattress stitch if preferred.

Collar

With RS facing and using smaller circular needle, beg and ending at left shoulder seam, pick up and knit 36 [36: 37: 39] sts down left side of neck, 12 sts from front, 36 [36: 37: 39] sts up right side of neck, then 32 [32: 34: 34] sts from back. 116 [116: 120: 124] sts.
Round 1 (RS of body, WS of collar): *K2, P2, rep from * to end.
This round forms rib.
Cont in rib until collar meas 13 cm.
Change to larger circular needle.
Cont in rib until collar meas 25 cm from pick-up round.
Cast off **loosely** in rib.
Cuffs (both alike)
With RS facing and using smaller needles, pick up and knit 138 [142: 146: 150] sts evenly along straight row-end edges of sleeve extensions.
Beg with row 2, work in rib as given for back for 14 rows, ending with **WS** facing for next row.
Cast off in rib (on **WS**).
See information page for finishing instructions.

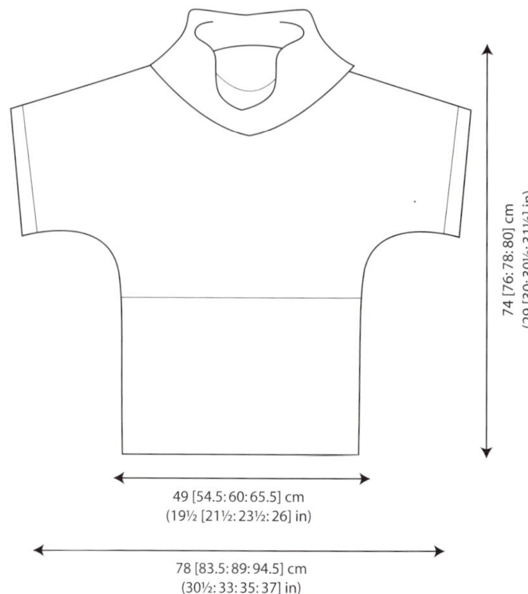

Main image page 18

 ## Logan

YARN

	S	M	L	XL	
To fit bust	81-86	91-97	102-107	112-117	cm
	32-34	36-38	40-42	44-46	in

Rowan RYC Cashmere Tweed

	14	16	18	20	x 25gm

(photographed in Iron 854)

Rowan RYC Wool Tweed

	7	8	9	10	x 50gm

NEEDLES

Cashmere Tweed version
1 pair 6mm (no 4) (US 10) needles

Wool Tweed version
1 pair 5½mm (no 5) (US 9) needles

TENSION

18 sts and 24 rows to 10 cm measured over pattern.

BODY (worked sideways, beg at one cuff edge)

Cast on 143 [147: 151: 155] sts.
Row 1 (RS): K1 [3: 1: 3], P1, *K3, P1, rep from * to last 1 [3: 1: 3] sts, K1 [3: 1: 3].
Row 2: K3 [1: 3: 1], P1, *K3, P1, rep from * to last 3 [1: 3: 1] sts, K3 [1: 3: 1].
These 2 rows form patt.
Cont in patt until work meas 17 [18: 19: 19] cm,

ending with RS facing for next row.
Shape for side seams
Inc 1 st at each end of next and foll 4 alt rows, then on foll 2 rows, taking inc sts into patt and ending with **WS** facing for next row.
157 [161: 165: 169] sts.
Cast on 5 sts at beg of next 4 rows, then 5 [7: 8: 10] sts at beg of foll 2 rows.
187 [195: 201: 209] sts.
Cont straight until work meas 5 [7.5: 10: 13] cm from last set of cast-on sts, ending with RS facing for next row.
Divide for neck
Next row (RS): Patt 93 [97: 100: 104] sts and turn, leaving rem sts on a holder.
Work each side of neck separately.
Cont straight until work meas 30 [30: 31: 31] cm from dividing row, ending with **WS** facing for next row.
Break yarn and leave sts on a holder.
With RS facing, rejoin yarn to rem sts, work 2 tog, patt to end. 93 [97: 100: 104] sts.
Cont straight until work meas 30 [30: 31: 31] cm from dividing row, ending with **WS** facing for next row.
Join sections
Next row (WS): Patt 92 [96: 99: 103] sts of second section, inc in last st, then patt 93 [97: 100: 104] sts of first section. 187 [195: 201: 209] sts.
Cont straight until work meas 5 [7.5: 10: 13] cm from joining row, ending with RS facing for

next row.
Shape for side seams
Keeping patt correct, cast off 5 [7: 8: 10] sts at beg of next 2 rows, then 5 sts at beg of foll 4 rows.
157 [161: 165: 169] sts.
Dec 1 st at each end of next 3 rows, then on foll 4 alt rows. 143 [147: 151: 155] sts.
Cont straight until work meas 17 [18: 19: 19] cm from last dec, ending with RS facing for next row.
Cast off in patt.

MAKING UP

Press as described on the information page.
Join both side and underarm seams using back stitch, or mattress stitch if preferred.
See information page for finishing instructions.

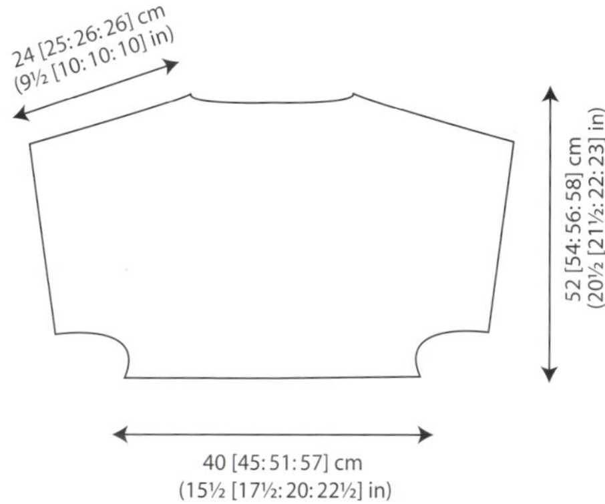

George

YARN

	S	M	L	XL	XXL	
To fit chest	102	107	112	117	122	cm
	40	42	44	46	48	in

Rowan RYC Cashmere Tweed

| | 55 | 58 | 60 | 64 | 68 | x 25gm |

Rowan RYC Wool Tweed

| | 27 | 28 | 29 | 31 | 33 | x 50gm |

(photographed in Ottoman 959)

NEEDLES

Cashmere Tweed version
1 pair 5mm (no 6) (US 8) needles
1 pair 6mm (no 4) (US 10) needles
Cable needle

Wool Tweed version
1 pair 4½mm (no 7) (US 7) needles
1 pair 5½mm (no 5) (US 9) needles
Cable needle

BUTTONS – 6 x 00345

TENSION

26 sts and 24 rows to 10 cm measured over
pattern using larger needles.

SPECIAL ABBREVIATIONS

Cr3R = slip next st onto cable needle and leave at
back of work, K2, then P1 from cable needle;
Cr3L = slip next 2 sts onto cable needle and leave
at front of work, P1, then K2 from cable needle;
C4B = slip next 2 sts onto cable needle and leave
at back of work, K2, then K2 from cable needle;
C4F = slip next 2 sts onto cable needle and leave
at front of work, K2, then K2 from cable needle;
Cr5R = slip next 2 sts onto cable needle and
leave at back of work, K3, then P2 from cable
needle; **Cr5L** = slip next 3 sts onto cable needle
and leave at front of work, P2, then K3 from cable
needle; **C6B** = slip next 3 sts onto cable needle
and leave at back of work, K3, then K3 from cable
needle; **C6F** = slip next 3 sts onto cable needle
and leave at front of work, K3, then K3 from cable

needle; **bind 3** = keeping yarn at back (WS) of
work, sl 1, K1, yfwd, K1, lift 4th st (the slipped st)
on right needle over first, 2nd and 3rd sts and off
right needle.

BACK

Using smaller needles cast on 104 [110: 114: 120:
126] sts.
Row 1 (RS): P1 [0: 0: 1: 0], K2 [2: 0: 2: 2], *P2, K2,
rep from * to last 1 [0: 2: 1: 0] sts, P1 [0: 2: 1: 0].
Row 2: K1 [0: 0: 1: 0], P2 [2: 0: 2: 2], *K2, P2, rep
from * to last 1 [0: 2: 1: 0] sts, K1 [0: 2: 1: 0].
These 2 rows form rib.
Work in rib for a further 15 rows, ending with **WS**
facing for next row.
Row 18 (WS): Rib 16 [19: 21: 24: 27], *M1, rib 2,
(M1, rib 1) twice, M1, rib 2, M1*, **rib 3, (M1, rib 1)
6 times, M1, rib 4, (M1, rib 1) 6 times, M1, rib 3**,
rep from * to * once more, rib 4, rep from * to *
once more, rep from ** to ** once more, rep from
* to * once more, rib to end.
152 [158: 162: 168: 174] sts.
Change to 6mm (US 10) needles.
Beg and ending rows as indicated and repeating
the 24 row patt repeat throughout, work in patt
from chart for body as folls:
Work straight until back meas 43 [44: 43: 44: 43]
cm, ending with RS facing for next row.
Shape armholes
Keeping patt correct, cast off 6 sts at beg of next
2 rows. 140 [146: 150: 156: 162] sts.
Dec 1 st at each end of next 5 [5: 5: 3: 3] rows,
then on foll 3 [2: 1: 2: 2] alt rows, then on 2 foll
4th rows. 120 [128: 134: 142: 148] sts.
Cont straight until armhole meas 23 [24: 25:
26: 27] cm, ending with RS facing for next row.
Shape shoulders and back neck
Cast off 12 [13: 14: 15: 16] sts at beg of next 2 rows.
96 [102: 106: 112: 116] sts.
Next row (RS): Cast off 12 [13: 14: 15: 16] sts, patt
until there are 16 [18: 18: 20: 20] sts on right
needle and turn, leaving rem sts on a holder.
Work each side of neck separately.
Cast off 4 sts at beg of next row.
Cast off rem 12 [14: 14: 16: 16] sts.

With RS facing, rejoin yarn to rem sts, cast off
centre 40 [40: 42: 42: 44] sts, patt to end.
Complete to match first side, reversing shapings.

LEFT FRONT

Using smaller needles cast on 53 [56: 58:
61: 64] sts.
Row 1 (RS): P1 [0: 0: 1: 0], K2 [2: 0: 2: 2], *P2, K2,
rep from * to last 2 sts, P2.
Row 2: *K2, P2, rep from * to last 1 [0: 2: 1: 0] sts,
K1 [0: 2: 1: 0].
These 2 rows form rib.
Work in rib for a further 15 rows, ending with **WS**
facing for next row.
Row 18 (WS): Rib 3, *M1, rib 2, (M1, rib 1) twice,
M1, rib 2, M1*, rib 3, (M1, rib 1) 6 times, M1, rib 4,
(M1, rib 1) 6 times, M1, rib 3, rep from * to * once
more, rib to end. 77 [80: 82: 85: 88] sts.
Change to 6mm (US 10) needles.
Beg and ending rows as indicated, work in patt
from chart for body as folls:
Work straight until left front matches back to beg
of armhole shaping, ending with RS facing for
next row.
Shape armhole
Keeping patt correct, cast off 6 sts at beg of next
row. 71 [74: 76: 79: 82] sts.
Work 1 row.
Dec 1 st at armhole edge of next 5 [5: 5: 3: 3] rows,
then on foll 3 [2: 1: 2: 2] alt rows, then on 2 foll
4th rows. 61 [65: 68: 72: 75] sts.
Cont straight until 15 [15: 17: 17: 19] rows less have
been worked than on back to beg of shoulder
shaping, ending with **WS** facing for next row.
Shape neck
Keeping patt correct, cast off 10 sts at beg of next
and foll alt row. 41 [45: 48: 52: 55] sts.
Dec 1 st at neck edge of next and foll 3 [3: 4: 4: 5]
alt rows, then on foll 4th row.
36 [40: 42: 46: 48] sts.
Work 1 row, ending with RS facing for next row.
Shape shoulder
Cast off 12 [13: 14: 15: 16] sts at beg of next and
foll alt row.
Work 1 row.

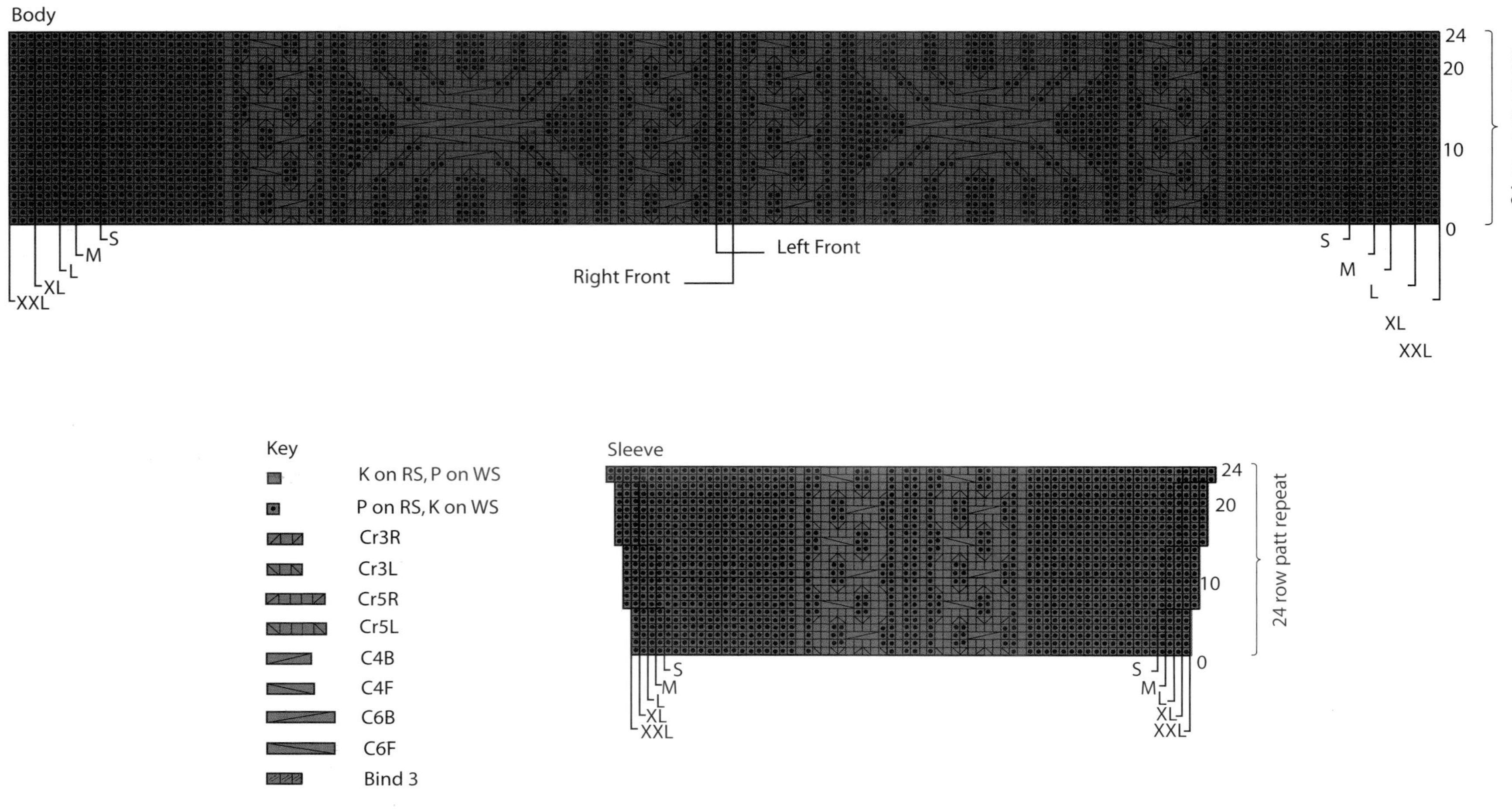

Body
24 row patt repeat
24
20
10
0
S
M
L
XL
XXL
Left Front
Right Front
S
M
L
XL
XXL
Key
K on RS, P on WS
P on RS, K on WS
Cr3R
Cr3L
Cr5R
Cr5L
C4B
C4F
C6B
C6F
Bind 3
Sleeve
24 row patt repeat
24
20
10
0
S
M
L
XL
XXL
S
M
L
XL
XXL

Cast off rem 12 [14: 14: 16: 16] sts.

RIGHT FRONT

Using smaller needles cast on 53 [56: 58: 61: 64] sts.

Row 1 (RS): *P2, K2, rep from * to last 1 [0: 2: 1: 0] sts, P1 [0: 2: 1: 0].

Row 2: K1 [0: 0: 1: 0], P2 [2: 0: 2: 2], *K2, P2, rep from * to last 2 sts, K2.

These 2 rows form rib.

Work in rib for a further 15 rows, ending with **WS** facing for next row.

Row 18 (WS): Rib 16 [19: 21: 24: 27], *M1, rib 2, (M1, rib 1) twice, M1, rib 2, M1*, rib 3, (M1, rib 1) 6 times, M1, rib 4, (M1, rib 1) 6 times, M1, rib 3, rep from * to * once more, rib 3.
77 [80: 82: 85: 88] sts.

Change to 6mm (US 10) needles.

Beg and ending rows as indicated, complete to match left front, reversing shapings.

SLEEVES

Using smaller needles cast on 50 [52: 54: 56: 58] sts.

Row 1 (RS): P0 [0: 0: 1: 0], K0 [1: 2: 2: 0], *P2, K2, rep from * to last 2 [3: 0: 1: 2] sts, P2 [2: 0: 1: 2], K0 [1: 0: 0: 0].

Row 2: K0 [0: 0: 1: 0], P0 [1: 2: 2: 0], *K2, P2, rep from * to last 2 [3: 0: 1: 2] sts, K2 [2: 0: 1: 2], P0 [1: 0: 0: 0].

These 2 rows form rib.

Work in rib for a further 15 rows, ending with **WS** facing for next row.

Row 18 (WS): Rib 17 [18: 19: 20: 21], *M1, rib 2, (M1, rib 1) twice, M1, rib 2, M1*, rib 4, rep from * to * once more, rib to end. 60 [62: 64: 66: 68] sts.
Change to 6mm (US 10) needles.

Beg and ending rows as indicated and repeating the 24 row patt repeat throughout, work in patt from chart for sleeve as folls:

Inc 1 st at each end of 7th and every foll 8th row to 84 [84: 84: 82: 82] sts, then on every foll – [10th: 10th: 10th: 10th] row until there are

- [86: 88: 90: 92] sts, taking inc sts into rev st st.
Cont straight until sleeve meas 52 [54: 56: 58: 60] cm, ending with RS facing for next row.

Shape top

Keeping patt correct, cast off 6 sts at beg of next 2 rows. 72 [74: 76: 78: 80] sts.

Dec 1 st at each end of next 5 rows, then on foll 3 alt rows, then on every foll 4th row until 50 [52: 54: 56: 58] sts rem.

Work 1 row.

Dec 1 st at each end of next and every foll alt row to 40 sts, then on foll row, ending with RS facing for next row. 38 sts.

Cast off 5 sts at beg of next 2 rows.

Cast off rem 28 sts.

MAKING UP

Press as described on the information page.

Join both shoulder seams using back stitch, or mattress stitch if preferred.

Collar

With RS facing and using smaller needles, beg and ending at front opening edges, pick up and knit 30 [30: 31: 33: 34] sts up right side of neck, 34 [34: 36: 36: 38] sts from back, then 30 [30: 31: 33: 34] sts down left side of neck. 94 [94: 98: 102: 106] sts.

Row 1 (RS of collar, WS of body): K2, *P2, K2, rep from * to end.

Row 2: P2, *K2, P2, rep from * to end.

These 2 rows form rib.

Cont in rib until collar meas 9 cm from pick-up row.
Cast off in rib.

Collar bands (both alike)

With RS of collar (**WS** of body) facing and using smaller needles, pick up and knit 20 sts along row-end edge of collar, between cast-off edge and pick-up row.

Row 1 (WS): K3, *P2, K2, rep from * to last st, K1.
Row 2: K1, P2, *K2, P2, rep from * to last st, K1.
These 2 rows form rib.

Work in rib for a further 8 rows, ending with **WS** of collar facing for next row.

Cast off in rib (on **WS**).

Button band

With RS of body facing and using smaller needles, pick up and knit 136 [140: 136: 140: 140] sts up right front opening edge, from cast-on edge to collar pick-up row.

Work in rib as given for collar band for 10 rows, ending with **WS** facing for next row.

Cast off in rib (on **WS**).

Buttonhole band

Work to match button band, picking up sts down left front opening edge and with the addition of 6 buttonholes worked in row 6 as folls:

Row 6 (RS): Rib 4, *cast off 2 sts (to make a buttonhole – cast on 2 sts over these cast-off sts on next row), rib until there are 23 [24: 23: 24: 24] sts on right needle after cast-off, rep from * 4 times more, cast off 2 sts (to make 6th buttonhole), rib to end.

Join ends of collar bands to ends of front bands at neck edge.

See information page for finishing instructions, setting in sleeves using the set-in method.

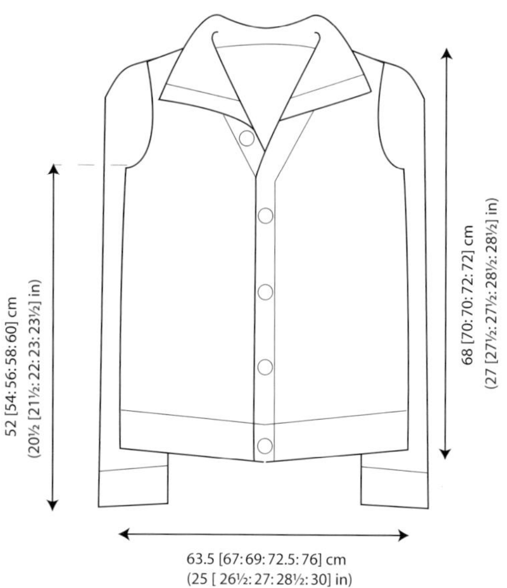

Main image page 21

 ## Glen mitts

YARN
Rowan RYC Cashmere Tweed
       2   x 25gm
(photographed in Iron 854)

Rowan RYC Wool Tweed
       1   x 50gm

NEEDLES
Cashmere Tweed version
1 pair 6mm (no 4) (US 10) needles

Cashmere Tweed version
1 pair 5½mm (no 5) (US 9) needles

TENSION
21 sts and 24 rows to 10 cm measured over rib.

RIGHT MITT
Cast on 54 sts.
Row 1 (RS): K2, *P2, K2, rep from * to end.
Row 2: P2, *K2, P2, rep from * to end.
These 2 rows form rib.
Cont in rib until mitt meas 11 cm, ending with RS facing for next row.
Shape thumb gusset
Keeping rib correct, cont as folls:
Row 1 (RS): Rib 27, place marker on needle, M1, rib 2, M1, place marker on needle, rib 25. 56 sts.
Keeping sts either side of markers correct in rib as set, and taking inc sts between markers into rib as set by the sts already between markers, cont as folls:
Work 3 rows.
Row 5: Rib 27, slip marker onto right needle, M1, rib 4, M1, slip marker onto right needle, rib 25. 58 sts.
Work 3 rows.
Row 9: Rib 27, slip marker onto right needle, M1, rib 6, M1, slip marker onto right needle, rib 25. 60 sts.
Work 3 rows.
Row 13: Rib 27, slip marker onto right needle, M1, rib 8, M1, slip marker onto right needle, rib 25. 62 sts.
Work 1 row.
Row 15: Rib 27, slip marker onto right needle, M1, rib 10, M1, slip marker onto right needle, rib 25. 64 sts.
Work 1 row.
Row 17: Rib 39, turn and cast on one st.
****Row 18:** Rib 13, turn and cast on one st.
Work 6 rows on these 14 sts only for thumb, ending with RS facing for next row.
Cast off.
Join thumb seam.
With RS facing, rejoin yarn, pick up and knit 6 sts from base of thumb, rib to end. 58 sts.
Cont in rib until mitt meas 24 cm from cast-on edge, ending with RS facing for next row.
Cast off in rib.

LEFT MITT
Work as given for right mitt to beg of thumb gusset shaping.
Shape thumb gusset
Keeping rib correct, cont as folls:
Row 1 (RS): Rib 25, place marker on needle, M1, rib 2, M1, place marker on needle, rib 27. 56 sts.
Keeping sts either side of markers correct in rib as set, and taking inc sts between markers into rib as set by the sts already between markers, cont as folls:
Work 3 rows.
Row 5: Rib 25, slip marker onto right needle, M1, rib 4, M1, slip marker onto right needle, rib 27. 58 sts.
Work 3 rows.
Row 9: Rib 25, slip marker onto right needle, M1, rib 6, M1, slip marker onto right needle, rib 27. 60 sts.
Work 3 rows.
Row 13: Rib 25, slip marker onto right needle, M1, rib 8, M1, slip marker onto right needle, rib 27. 62 sts.
Work 1 row.
Row 15: Rib 25, slip marker onto right needle, M1, rib 10, M1, slip marker onto right needle, rib 27. 64 sts.
Work 1 row.
Row 17: Rib 37, turn and cast on one st.
Complete as given for right mitt from **.

MAKING UP
Press as described on the information page.
Join side seam.

Main images page 20

Glen hat

YARN

	lady	man
Rowan RYC Cashmere Tweed	2	2	x 25gm

(lady's photographed in Tapestry 856, man's in Iron 854)

Rowan RYC Wool Tweed
1   1   x 50gm

NEEDLES
Cashmere Tweed version
1 pair 6mm (no 4) (US 10) needles

Wool Tweed version
1 pair 5½mm (no 5) (US 9) needles

TENSION
21 sts and 24 rows to 10 cm measured over rib.

HAT
Cast on 102 [106] sts.
Row 1 (RS): K2, *P2, K2, rep from * to end.
Row 2: P2, *K2, P2, rep from * to end.
These 2 rows form rib.
Cont in rib until hat meas 13 [14] cm, ending with RS facing for next row.
Shape crown
Row 1 (RS): K2, (P2, K2tog) 25 [26] times. 77 [80] sts.
Row 2: (P1, K2) 25 [26] times, P2.
Row 3: K2, (P2, K1) 25 [26] times.
Rows 4 and 5: As rows 2 and 3.

Row 6: As row 2.
Row 7: K2tog, (P1, K2tog) 25 [26] times. 51 [53] sts.
Row 8: P1, *K1, P1, rep from * to end.
Row 9: K1, *P1, K1, rep from * to end.
Rows 10 and 11: As rows 8 and 9.
Row 12: As row 8.
Row 13: (K3tog, P1) 12 [13] times, (K3tog) 1 [0] times, K0 [1]. 25 [27] sts.
Row 14: As row 8.
Row 15: K1, (K2tog) 12 [13] times.
Break yarn and thread through rem 13 [14] sts.
Pull up tight and fasten off securely.

MAKING UP
Press as described on the information page.
Join back seam.

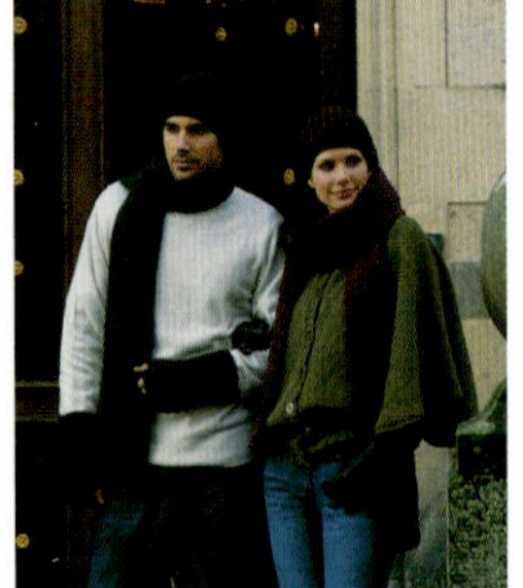

Main image page 20

Glen scarf

YARN

	lady	man
Rowan RYC Cashmere Tweed	15	21	x 25gm
Rowan RYC Wool Tweed	7	10	x 50gm

(lady's photographed in Ottoman 959, man's in Mull 955)

NEEDLES
Cashmere Tweed version
1 pair 6mm (no 4) (US 10) needles
Wool Tweed version
1 pair 5½mm (no 5) (US 9) needlesTENSION
21 sts and 24 rows to 10 cm measured over rib.

FINISHED SIZE
Completed scarf measures 18 [20] cm (7 [8] in) wide and 300 [180] cm (118 [71] in) long.

SCARF
Cast on 38 [42] sts.
Row 1 (RS): K2, *P2, K2, rep from * to end.
Row 2: P2, *K2, P2, rep from * to end.
These 2 rows form rib.
Cont in rib until scarf meas 300 [180] cm, ending with RS facing for next row.
Cast off in rib.

MAKING UP
Press as described on the information page.

Main image page 26

 **Iona**

YARN

	8	10	12	14	16	18	20	22	
To fit bust	81	86	91	97	102	107	112	117	cm
	32	34	36	38	40	42	44	46	in

Rowan RYC Cashmere Tweed

16 16 17 18 19 20 21 22 x 25gm
(photographed in Pewter 853)

Rowan RYC Wool Tweed

8 8 9 9 10 10 11 11 x 50gm

NEEDLES
Cashmere Tweed version
1 pair 5mm (no 6) (US 8) needles
1 pair 6mm (no 4) (US 10) needles
5mm (no 6) (US 8) circular needle
2 double-pointed 5mm (no 6) (US 8) needles

Wool Tweed version
1 pair 4½mm (no 7) (US 7) needles
1 pair 5½mm (no 5) (US 9) needles
1 pair 4½mm (no 7) (US 7) circular needle
2 double-pointed 4½mm (no 7) (US 7) needles

TENSION
18 sts and 24 rows to 10 cm measured over
stocking stitch using larger needles.

BACK
Using smaller needles cast on 81 [85: 89: 93: 99:
105: 111: 115] sts.
Beg with a K row, work in st st for 5 rows, ending
with **WS** facing for next row.
Row 6 (WS): Knit (to form fold line).
Change to 6mm (US 10) needles.**
Beg with a K row, work in st st until back meas
38 [38: 37: 40: 39: 41: 40: 42] cm **from fold line
row**, ending with RS facing for next row.
Shape armholes
Cast off 5 [6: 6: 7: 7: 8: 8: 9] sts at beg of next
2 rows. 71 [73: 77: 79: 85: 89: 95: 97] sts.
Dec 1 st at each end of next 3 [3: 5: 5: 7: 7: 9: 9]
rows, then on foll 3 [3: 2: 2: 1: 2: 2: 1] alt rows,
then on foll 4th row.
57 [59: 61: 63: 67: 69: 71: 75] sts.

Cont straight until armhole meas 20 [20: 21: 21: 22:
22: 23: 23] cm, ending with RS facing for next row.
Shape shoulders and back neck
Cast off 5 [5: 6: 6: 6: 7: 7: 8] sts at beg of next
2 rows. 47 [49: 49: 51: 55: 55: 57: 59] sts.
Next row (RS): Cast off 5 [5: 6: 6: 6: 7: 7: 8] sts,
K until there are 9 [10: 9: 10: 11: 10: 11: 11] sts on
right needle and turn, leaving rem sts on a holder.
Work each side of neck separately.
Cast off 4 sts at beg of next row.
Cast off rem 5 [6: 5: 6: 7: 6: 7: 7] sts.
With RS facing, rejoin yarn to rem sts, cast off
centre 19 [19: 19: 19: 21: 21: 21: 21] sts, K to end.
Complete to match first side, reversing shapings.

FRONT
Work as given for back to **.
Beg with a K row, work in st st for 2 rows, ending
with RS facing for next row.
Row 9 (RS): K37 [39: 41: 43: 46: 49: 52: 54],
K2tog, yfwd, K3, yfwd, sl 1, K1, psso, K to end.
Beg with a P row, work in st st until 40 rows less
have been worked than on back to beg of armhole
shaping, ending with RS facing for next row.
Divide for neck
Next row (RS): K40 [42: 44: 46: 49: 52: 55: 57]
and turn, leaving rem sts on a holder.
Work each side of neck separately.
Dec 1 st at neck edge of 6th and 5 foll 6th rows.
34 [36: 38: 40: 43: 46: 49: 51] sts.
Work 3 rows, ending with RS facing for next row.
Shape armhole
Cast off 5 [6: 6: 7: 7: 8: 8: 9] sts at beg of next
row. 29 [30: 32: 33: 36: 38: 41: 42] sts.
Work 1 row.
Dec 1 st at armhole edge of next 3 [3: 5: 5: 7: 7:
9: 9] rows, then on foll 3 [3: 2: 2: 1: 2: 2: 1] alt
rows, then on foll 4th row **and at same time** dec
1 st at neck edge of next and every foll 6th row.
19 [20: 21: 22: 24: 25: 26: 28] sts.
Dec 1 st at neck edge **only** on 6th [6th: 6th: 6th:
6th: 4th: 2nd: 4th] and 2 [2: 1: 1: 4: 4: 2: 2] foll 6th
rows, then on 1 [1: 2: 2: 0: 0: 2: 2] foll 8th rows.
15 [16: 17: 18: 19: 20: 21: 23] sts.
Cont straight until front matches back to beg of

shoulder shaping, ending with RS facing for next
row.
Shape shoulder
Cast off 5 [5: 6: 6: 6: 7: 7: 8] sts at beg of next
and foll alt row.
Work 1 row.
Cast off rem 5 [6: 5: 6: 7: 6: 7: 7] sts.
With RS facing, slip centre st onto a holder, rejoin
yarn to rem sts, K to end.
Complete to match first side, reversing shapings.

SLEEVES
Using smaller needles cast on 42 [42: 46: 46: 46:
46: 50: 50] sts.
Row 1 (RS): K2, *P2, K2, rep from * to end.
Row 2: P2, *K2, P2, rep from * to end.
These 2 rows form rib.
Work in rib for a further 16 rows, inc [inc: dec:
dec: inc: inc: dec: dec] 1 st at end of last row and
ending with RS facing for next row.
43 [43: 45: 45: 47: 47: 49: 49] sts.
Change to larger needles.
Beg with a K row, work in st st, shaping sides by
inc 1 st at each end of 9th [9th: 9th: 7th: 7th: 7th:
7th: 5th] and every foll 12th [10th: 10th: 8th: 8th:
8th: 8th: 6th] row to 57 [57: 57: 51: 51: 61: 65: 53]
sts, then on every foll - [12th: 12th: 10th: 10th:
10th: 10th: 8th] row until there are - [59: 61: 63:
65: 67: 69: 71] sts.
Cont straight until sleeve meas 45 [45: 46: 46: 47:
47: 46: 46] cm, ending with RS facing for next row.
Shape top
Cast off 5 [6: 6: 7: 7: 8: 8: 9] sts at beg of next
2 rows. 47 [47: 49: 49: 51: 51: 53: 53] sts.
Dec 1 st at each end of next 3 rows, then on foll
3 alt rows, then on every foll 4th row until 25 [25:
27: 27: 29: 29: 31: 31] sts rem.
Work 1 row, ending with RS facing for next row.
Dec 1 st at each end of next and every foll alt row
to 21 sts, then on foll row, ending with RS facing
for next row.
Cast off rem 19 sts.

MAKING UP
Press as described on the information page.

Join both shoulder seams using back stitch, or mattress stitch if preferred.

Neckband

With RS facing and using circular needle, beg and ending at left shoulder seam, pick up and knit 92 [92: 92: 92: 96: 96: 96: 96] sts down left side of neck, K st left on holder at base of V and mark this st with a coloured thread, pick up and knit 92 [92: 92: 92: 96: 96: 96: 96] sts up right side of neck, then 26 [26: 26: 26: 30: 30: 30: 30] sts from back. 211 [211: 211: 211: 223: 223: 223: 223] sts.

Round 1 (RS): *K2, P2, rep from * to within 4 sts of marked st, K2, K2tog tbl, K marked st, K2tog, **K2, P2, rep from ** to end.

This round sets position of rib.

Keeping rib correct, cont as folls:

Round 2: Rib to within 2 sts of marked st, K2tog tbl, K marked st, K2tog, rib to end.

Rep last round 6 times more. 195 [195: 195: 195: 207: 207: 207: 207] sts.

Cast off in rib, still decreasing either side of marked st as before.

Tie

Using double-pointed needles cast on 3 sts.

Row 1 (RS): K3, *without turning slip these 3 sts to opposite end of needle and bring yarn to opposite end of work pulling it quite tightly across **WS** of work, K these 3 sts again, rep from * until tie is 145 [150: 155: 160: 165: 170: 175: 180] cm long.

Cast off.

See information page for finishing instructions, setting in sleeves using the set-in method. Fold first 5 rows to inside around lower edge and slip stitch in place. Thread tie through this casing, passing it through eyelet holes of row 9 of front, and tie ends at centre front.

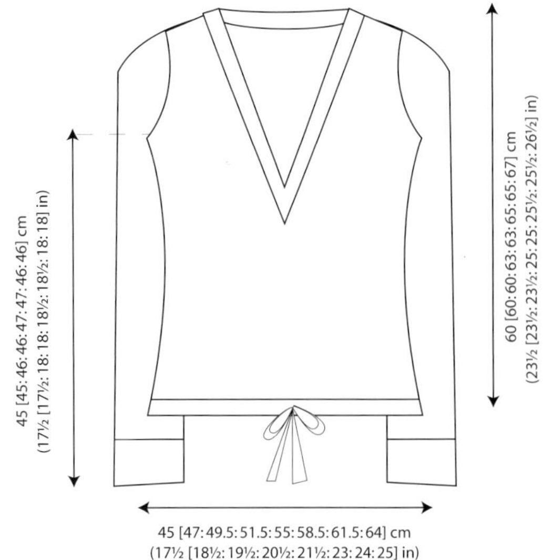

Main image page 14

Lewis [ladies version]

YARN

	8	10	12	14	16	18	20	22	
To fit bust	81	86	91	97	102	107	112	117	cm
	32	34	36	38	40	42	44	46	in

Rowan RYC Cashmere Tweed

	17	18	18	20	21	22	23	24 x 25gm

(photographed in Flannel 851)

Rowan RYC Wool Tweed

	9	9	9	10	11	11	12	12 x 50gm

NEEDLES
Cashmere Tweed version
1 pair 5mm (no 6) (US 8) needles
1 pair 6mm (no 4) (US 10) needles
5mm (no 6) (US 8) circular needle
Wool Tweed version
1 pair 4½mm (no 7) (US 7) needles
1 pair 5½mm (no 5) (US 9) needles
1 pair 4½mm (no 7) (US 7) circular needle

TENSION
17 sts and 35 rows to 10 cm measured over garter stitch using larger needles.

BACK
Using smaller needles cast on 78 [82: 86: 90: 98: 102: 110: 114] sts.
Row 1 (RS): K2, *P2, K2, rep from * to end.
Row 2: P2, *K2, P2, rep from * to end.
These 2 rows form rib.
Work in rib for a further 15 rows, ending with **WS** facing for next row.
Row 18 (WS): Rib 8 [8: 9: 9: 8: 7: 5: 7], work 2 tog, (rib 18 [19: 20: 21: 14: 15: 12: 12], work 2 tog) 3 [3: 3: 3: 5: 5: 7: 7] times, rib to end.
74 [78: 82: 86: 92: 96: 102: 106] sts.

Change to larger needles.
Work in g st, shaping side seams by dec 1 st at each end of 13th and foll 10th row, then on foll 8th row, then on foll 6th row.
66 [70: 74: 78: 84: 88: 94: 98] sts.
Work 9 rows, ending with RS facing for next row.
Inc 1 st at each end of next and every foll 10th row until there are 74 [78: 82: 86: 92: 96: 102: 106] sts.
Cont straight until back meas 33 [33: 32: 35: 34: 36: 35: 37] cm, ending with RS facing for next row.
Shape raglan armholes
Cast off 5 sts at beg of next 2 rows.
64 [68: 72: 76: 82: 86: 92: 96] sts.
Dec 1 st at each end of next and foll 1 [5: 7: 11: 13: 17: 21: 25] alt rows, then on every foll 4th row until 24 [24: 24: 24: 26: 26: 26: 26] sts rem.
Work 3 rows, ending with RS facing for next row.
Cast off.

FRONT
Work as given for back until 38 [38: 38: 40: 42: 42: 44: 44] sts rem in raglan armhole shaping.
Work 3 rows, ending with RS facing for next row.
Shape neck
Next row (RS): K2tog, K12 [12: 12: 13: 14: 14: 15: 15] and turn, leaving rem sts on a holder.
Work each side of neck separately.
Dec 1 st at raglan armhole edge of 4th and 4 [4: 4: 5: 5: 5: 6: 6] foll 4th rows **and at same time** dec 1 st at neck edge of 2nd and foll 2 [2: 2: 0: 2: 2: 0: 0] alt rows, then on 3 [3: 3: 5: 4: 4: 6: 6] foll 4th rows. 2 sts.
Work 1 row, ending with RS facing for next row.
Next row (RS): K2tog and fasten off.
With RS facing, rejoin yarn to rem sts, cast off centre 10 sts, K to last 2 sts, K2tog.

Complete to match first side, reversing shapings.

SLEEVES
Using smaller needles cast on 42 [42: 46: 46: 46: 46: 50: 50] sts.
Work in rib as given for back for 17 rows, ending with **WS** facing for next row.
Row 18 (WS): Rib 9 [9: 4: 4: 10: 10: 6: 6], work 2 tog, (rib 19 [19: 10: 10: 21: 21: 10: 10], work 2 tog) 1 [1: 3: 3: 1: 1: 3: 3] times, rib to end.
40 [40: 42: 42: 44: 44: 46: 46] sts.
Change to larger needles.
Work in g st, shaping sides by inc 1 st at each end of 7th and every foll 8th row to 50 [50: 50: 50: 48: 48: 54: 54] sts, then on every foll 10th row until there are 66 [66: 68: 68: 70: 70: 72: 72] sts.
Cont straight until sleeve meas 45 [45: 46: 46: 47: 47: 46: 46] cm, ending with RS facing for next row.
Shape raglan
Cast off 5 sts at beg of next 2 rows.
56 [56: 58: 58: 60: 60: 62: 62] sts.
Dec 1 st at each end of next and foll 5 alt rows, then on every foll 4th row until 14 sts rem.
Work 1 row, ending with RS facing for next row.
Left sleeve only
Work 1 row.
Cast off 4 sts at beg of next row, then 3 sts at beg of foll 2 alt rows, ending with RS facing for next row, **and at same time** dec 1 st at beg of 2nd row.
Right sleeve only
Cast off 4 sts at beg of next row, then 3 sts at beg of foll 2 alt rows **and at same time** dec 1 st at end of 3rd row.
Work 1 row, ending with RS facing for next row.
Both sleeves
Cast off rem 3 sts.

MAKING UP
Press as described on the information page.
Join both front and both back raglan armhole
seams using back stitch, or mattress stitch if
preferred.

Neckband
With RS facing and using circular needle, beg and
ending at left back raglan seam, pick up and knit
9 sts from left sleeve, 15 [15: 15: 17: 18: 18: 20: 20]
sts down left side of neck, 10 sts from front, 15 [15:
15: 17: 18: 18: 20: 20] sts up right side of neck,
9 sts from right sleeve, then
26 [26: 26: 26: 28: 28: 28: 28] sts from back.
84 [84: 84: 88: 92: 92: 96: 96] sts.
Round 1 (RS): *K2, P2, rep from * to end.
Rep last round 7 times more.
Cast off in rib.
See information page for finishing instructions.

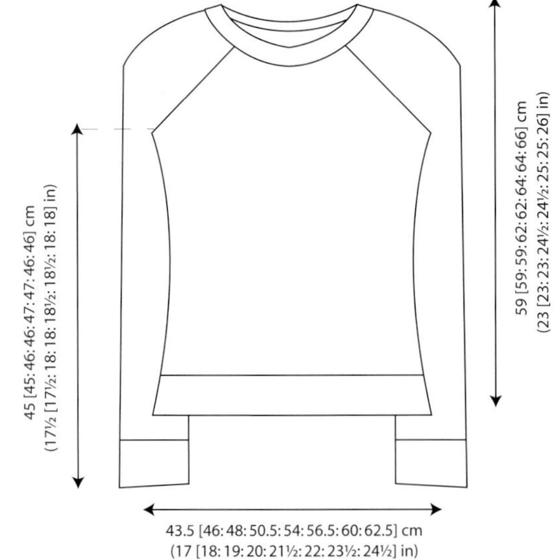

Main image page 32

Lewis [mens version]

YARN

	S	M	L	XL	XXL	
To fit chest	102	107	112	117	122	cm
	40	42	44	46	48	in

Rowan RYC Cashmere Tweed

| | 21 | 23 | 24 | 26 | 27 | x 50gm |

(photographed in Cambric 855)

Rowan RYC Wool Tweed

| | 11 | 12 | 12 | 13 | 14 | x 50gm |

NEEDLES

Cashmere Tweed version
1 pair 5mm (no 6) (US 8) needles
1 pair 6mm (no 4) (US 10) needles
5mm (no 6) (US 8) circular needle

Wool Tweed version
1 pair 4½mm (no 7) (US 7) needles
1 pair 5½mm (no 5) (US 9) needles
1 pair 4½mm (no 7) (US 7) circular needle

TENSION

17 sts and 35 rows to 10 cm measured over garter stitch using larger needles.

BACK

Using smaller needles cast on 102 [110: 114: 122: 126] sts.
Row 1 (RS): K2, *P2, K2, rep from * to end.
Row 2: P2, *K2, P2, rep from * to end.
These 2 rows form rib.
Work in rib for a further 15 rows, ending with **WS** facing for next row.

Row 18 (WS): Rib 11 [9: 8: 7: 6], work 2 tog, (rib 24 [16: 17: 13: 14], work 2 tog) 3 [5: 5: 7: 7] times, rib to end.
98 [104: 108: 114: 118] sts.
Change to larger needles.
Work in g st until back meas 38 [39: 38: 39: 38] cm, ending with RS facing for next row.
Shape raglan armholes
Cast off 5 sts at beg of next 2 rows.
88 [94: 98: 104: 108] sts.
Dec 1 st at each end of next and foll 14 [18: 18: 22: 22] alt rows, then on every foll 4th row until 26 [26: 28: 28: 30] sts rem.
Work 3 rows, ending with RS facing for next row.
Cast off.

FRONT

Work as given for back until 40 [40: 44: 44: 48] sts rem in raglan armhole shaping.
Work 3 rows, ending with RS facing for next row.
Shape neck
Next row (RS): K2tog, K12 [12: 14: 14: 16] and turn, leaving rem sts on a holder.
Work each side of neck separately.
Dec 1 st at raglan armhole edge of 4th and 4 [4: 5: 5: 6] foll 4th rows **and at same time** dec 1 st at neck edge of 2nd and foll 2 alt rows, then on 3 [3: 4: 4: 5] foll 4th rows. 2 sts.
Work 1 row, ending with RS facing for next row.
Next row (RS): K2tog and fasten off.
With RS facing, rejoin yarn to rem sts, cast off centre 12 sts, K to last 2 sts, K2tog.
Complete to match first side, reversing shapings.

SLEEVES

Using smaller needles cast on 46 [46: 50: 50: 54] sts.
Work in rib as given for back for 17 rows, ending with **WS** facing for next row.
Row 18 (WS): Rib 4 [10: 4: 11: 5], work 2 tog, (rib 10 [21: 11: 23: 12], work 2 tog) 3 [1: 3: 1: 3] times, rib to end. 42 [44: 46: 48: 50] sts.
Change to larger needles.
Work in g st, shaping sides by inc 1 st at each end of 5th [7th: 7th: 7th: 7th] and every foll 6th [8th: 8th: 8th: 8th] row to 46 [76: 72: 66: 62] sts, then on every foll 8th [10th: 10th: 10th: 10th] row until there are 78 [80: 82: 84: 86] sts.
Cont straight until sleeve meas 51 [53: 55: 57: 59] cm, ending with RS facing for next row.
Shape raglan
Cast off 5 sts at beg of next 2 rows.
68 [70: 72: 74: 76] sts.
Dec 1 st at each end of next and foll 14 alt rows, then on every foll 4th row until 8 sts rem.
Work 1 row, ending with RS facing for next row.
Left sleeve only
Place marker at beg of last row to denote front neck point.
Right sleeve only
Place marker at end of last row to denote front neck point.
Both sleeves
Dec 1 st at front neck edge of next 5 rows **and at same time** dec 1 st at back raglan armhole edge of 3rd row.
Work 1 row, ending with RS facing for next row.
Next row (RS): K2tog and fasten off.

MAKING UP

Press as described on the information page.
Join both front and both back raglan armhole
seams using back stitch, or mattress stitch if
preferred.

Neckband

With RS facing and using circular needle, beg and
ending at left back raglan seam, pick up and knit
8 sts from left sleeve, 16 [16: 17: 19: 20] sts down
left side of neck, 12 sts from front, 16 [16: 17:
19: 20] sts up right side of neck, 8 sts from right
sleeve, then 28 [28: 30: 30: 32] sts from back.
88 [88: 92: 96: 100] sts.

Round 1 (RS): *K2, P2, rep from * to end.
Rep last round 7 times more.
Cast off in rib.
See information page for finishing instructions.

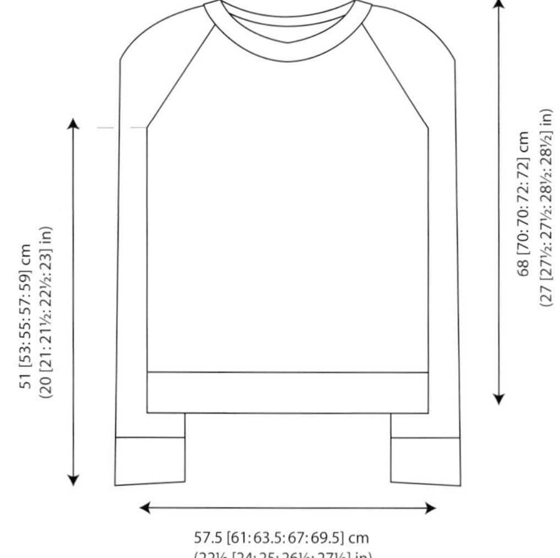

Main image page 12

 **Mac**

YARN

	S	M	L	XL	XXL	
To fit chest	102	107	112	117	122	cm
	40	42	44	46	48	in

Rowan RYC Cashmere Tweed

| | 34 | 37 | 39 | 42 | 44 | x 25gm |

Rowan RYC Wool Tweed

| | 17 | 19 | 20 | 21 | 22 | x 50gm |

(photographed in Mull 955)

NEEDLES

Cashmere Tweed version
1 pair 5mm (no 6) (US 8) needles
1 pair 6mm (no 4) (US 10) needles

Wool Tweed version
1 pair 4½mm (no 7) (US 7) needles
1 pair 5½mm (no 5) (US 9) needles

BUTTONS – 4 x 00340

TENSION

19 sts and 24 rows to 10 cm measured over pattern using larger needles.

BACK

Using smaller needles cast on 110 [116: 122: 128: 132] sts.
Row 1 (RS): P0 [2: 0: 0: 1], K3 [4: 0: 3: 4], *P5, K4, rep from * to last 8 [2: 5: 8: 1] sts, P5 [2: 5: 5: 1], K3 [0: 0: 3: 0].
Row 2: K0 [2: 0: 0: 1], P3 [4: 0: 3: 4], *K5, P4, rep from * to last 8 [2: 5: 8: 1] sts, K5 [2: 5: 5: 1], P3 [0: 0: 3: 0].
These 2 rows form patt.
Change to 6mm (US 10) needles.
Cont in patt until back meas 43 [44: 43: 44: 43] cm, ending with RS facing for next row.
Shape armholes
Keeping patt correct, cast off 7 sts at beg of next 2 rows. 96 [102: 108: 114: 118] sts.
Dec 1 st at each end of next 3 [3: 3: 3: 1] rows, then on foll 3 [2: 1: 1: 1] alt rows, then on foll 4th row. 82 [90: 98: 104: 112] sts.
Cont straight until armhole meas 23 [24: 25: 26: 27] cm, ending with RS facing for next row.

Shape shoulders and back neck
Cast off 8 [9: 10: 11: 12] sts at beg of next 2 rows. 66 [72: 78: 82: 88] sts.
Next row (RS): Cast off 8 [9: 10: 11: 12] sts, patt until there are 12 [14: 15: 16: 17] sts on right needle and turn, leaving rem sts on a holder.
Work each side of neck separately.
Cast off 4 sts at beg of next row.
Cast off rem 8 [10: 11: 12: 13] sts.
With RS facing, rejoin yarn to rem sts, cast off centre 26 [26: 28: 28: 30] sts, patt to end.
Complete to match first side, reversing shapings.

FRONT

Work as given for back until 20 rows less have been worked than on back to beg of armhole shaping, ending with RS facing for next row.
Divide for front opening
Next row (RS): Patt 51 [54: 57: 60: 62] sts and turn, leaving rem sts on a holder.
Work each side of neck separately.
Work 19 rows, ending with RS facing for next row.
Shape armhole
Keeping patt correct, cast off 7 sts at beg of next row. 44 [47: 50: 53: 55] sts.
Work 1 row.
Dec 1 st at armhole edge of next 3 [3: 3: 3: 1] rows, then on foll 3 [2: 1: 1: 1] alt rows, then on foll 4th row. 37 [41: 45: 48: 52] sts.
Cont straight until 15 [15: 17: 17: 19] rows less have been worked than on back to beg of shoulder shaping, ending with **WS** facing for next row.
Shape neck
Keeping patt correct, cast off 6 sts at beg of next row. 31 [35: 39: 42: 46] sts.
Dec 1 st at neck edge of next 3 rows, then on foll 3 [3: 4: 4: 5] alt rows, then on foll 4th row. 24 [28: 31: 34: 37] sts.
Work 1 row, ending with RS facing for next row.
Shape shoulder
Cast off 8 [9: 10: 11: 12] sts at beg of next and foll alt row.
Work 1 row.
Cast off rem 8 [10: 11: 12: 13] sts.
With RS facing, rejoin yarn to rem sts, cast off centre 8 sts, patt to end.
Complete to match first side, reversing shapings.

SLEEVES

Using smaller needles cast on 48 [50: 52: 54: 56] sts.
Row 1 (RS): P4 [0: 0: 0: 0], K4 [0: 1: 2: 3], *P5, K4, rep from * to last 4 [5: 6: 7: 8] sts, P4 [5: 5: 5: 5], K0 [0: 1: 2: 3].
Row 2: K4 [0: 0: 0: 0], P4 [0: 1: 2: 3], *K5, P4, rep from * to last 4 [5: 6: 7: 8] sts, K4 [5: 5: 5: 5], P0 [0: 1: 2: 3].
These 2 rows form patt.
Change to larger needles.
Cont in patt, shaping sides by inc 1 st at each end of 3rd [3rd: 5th: 5th: 5th] and every foll 6th [6th: 8th: 8th: 8th] row to 56 [54: 82: 80: 78] sts, then on every foll 8th [8th: -: 10th: 10th] row until there are 78 [80: -: 84: 86] sts, taking inc sts into patt.
Cont straight until sleeve meas 52 [54: 56: 58: 60] cm, ending with RS facing for next row.
Shape top
Keeping patt correct, cast off 7 sts at beg of next 2 rows. 64 [66: 68: 70: 72] sts.
Dec 1 st at each end of next 3 rows, then on foll 3 alt rows, then on every foll 4th row until 46 [48: 50: 52: 54] sts rem.
Work 1 row.
Dec 1 st at each end of next and every foll alt row to 36 sts, then on foll 3 rows, ending with RS facing for next row. 30 sts.
Cast off 5 sts at beg of next 2 rows.
Cast off rem 20 sts.

MAKING UP

Press as described on the information page.
Join both shoulder seams using back stitch, or mattress stitch if preferred.
Collar
With RS facing and using smaller needles, beg and ending at front opening edges, pick up and knit 26 [26: 27: 29: 30] sts up right side of neck, 34 [34: 36: 36: 38] sts from back, then 26 [26: 27: 29: 30] sts down left side of neck. 86 [86: 90: 94: 98] sts.
Row 1 (RS of collar, WS of body): K2, *P2, K2, rep from * to end.
Row 2: P2, *K2, P2, rep from * to end.
These 2 rows form rib.
Cont in rib until collar meas 9 cm from pick-up row.

Cast off in rib.

Collar bands (both alike)

With RS of collar (**WS** of body) facing and using smaller needles, pick up and knit 20 sts along row-end edge of collar, between cast-off edge and pick-up row.

Row 1 (WS): K3, *P2, K2, rep from * to last st, K1.

Row 2: K1, P2, *K2, P2, rep from * to last st, K1.

These 2 rows form rib.

Work in rib for a further 8 rows, ending with **WS** of collar facing for next row.

Cast off in rib (on **WS**).

Button band

With RS of body facing and using smaller needles, pick up and knit 60 [60: 60: 64: 64] sts up right front opening edge, from base of front opening to collar pick-up row.

Work in rib as given for collar band for 10 rows, ending with **WS** facing for next row.

Cast off in rib (on **WS**).

Buttonhole band

Work to match button band, picking up sts down left front opening edge and with the addition of 4 buttonholes worked in row 6 as folls:

Row 6 (RS): Rib 4, *cast off 2 sts (to make a buttonhole – cast on 2 sts over these cast-off sts on next row), rib until there are 15 [15: 15: 16: 16] sts

on right needle after cast-off, rep from * twice more, cast off 2 sts (to make 4th buttonhole), rib to end.

Join ends of collar bands to ends of front bands at neck edge. Sew row-end edge of buttonhole

band to cast-off sts at base of front opening, then sew row-end edge of button band in place behind buttonhole band.

See information page for finishing instructions, setting in sleeves using the set-in method.

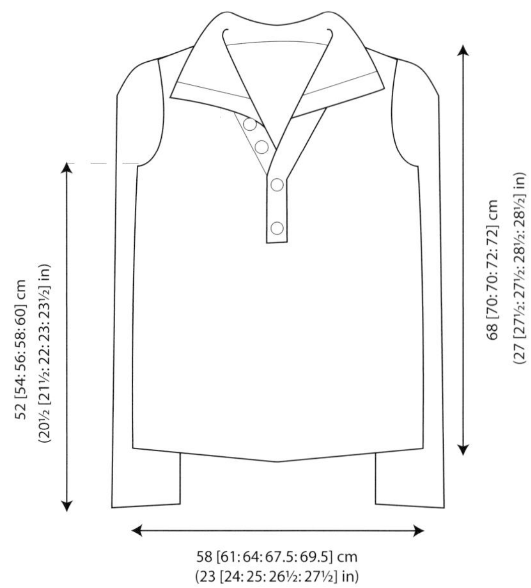

Main image page 34

Minna

YARN

	S	M	L	XL	
To fit bust	81-86	91-97	102-107	112-117	cm
	32-34	36-38	40-42	44-46	in

Rowan RYC Cashmere Tweed

	18	19	22	24	x 25gm

(photographed in Tapestry 856)

Rowan RYC Wool Tweed

	9	10	11	12	x 50gm

NEEDLES

Cashmere Tweed version
1 pair 5mm (no 6) (US 8) needles
1 pair 6mm (no 4) (US 10) needles

Wool Tweed version
1 pair 4½mm (no 7) (US 7) needles
1 pair 5½mm (no 5) (US 9) needles

RIBBON – 250 cm of 4 cm wide satin ribbon

TENSION

18 sts and 24 rows to 10 cm measured over
stocking stitch using 6mm (US 10) needles.

BACK

Using smaller needles cast on 85 [93: 105: 115] sts.
Work in g st for 2 rows, ending with RS facing for
next row.
Change to larger needles.
Beg with a K row, work in st st until back meas
38 [39: 40: 41] cm, ending with RS facing for next
row.
Shape armholes
Cast off 6 [7: 8: 9] sts at beg of next 2 rows.
73 [79: 89: 97] sts.
Dec 1 st at each end of next 3 [5: 7: 9] rows, then
on foll 3 [2: 2: 2] alt rows, then on foll 4th row.
59 [63: 69: 73] sts.
Cont straight until armhole meas 20 [21: 22: 23] cm,
ending with RS facing for next row.

Shape shoulders and back neck
Cast off 4 [5: 5: 6] sts at beg of next 2 rows.
51 [53: 59: 61] sts.
Next row (RS): Cast off 4 [5: 5: 6] sts, K until
there are 8 [8: 10: 10] sts on right needle and
turn, leaving rem sts on a holder.
Work each side of neck separately.
Cast off 4 sts at beg of next row.
Cast off rem 4 [4: 6: 6] sts.
With RS facing, rejoin yarn to rem sts, cast off
centre 27 [27: 29: 29] sts, K to end.
Complete to match first side, reversing shapings.

LEFT FRONT

Using smaller needles cast on 57 [61: 67: 72] sts.
Work in g st for 2 rows, ending with RS facing for
next row.
Change to larger needles.
Beg with a K row, work in st st until 16 rows less
have been worked than on back to beg of armhole
shaping, ending with RS facing for next row.
Shape front slope
Dec 1 st at end of next row and at same edge on
foll 14 rows. 42 [46: 52: 57] sts.
Work 1 row, ending with RS facing for next row.
Shape armhole
Cast off 6 [7: 8: 9] sts at beg and dec 1 st at end
of next row. 35 [38: 43: 47] sts.
Work 1 row.
Dec 1 st at armhole edge of next 3 [5: 7: 9] rows,
then on foll 3 [2: 2: 2] alt rows, then on foll 4th
row **and at same time** dec 1 st at front slope edge
on next and every foll alt row. 21 [23: 25: 26] sts.
Dec 1 st at front slope edge **only** on 2nd and foll
4 [3: 3: 0] alt rows, then on every foll 4th row
until 12 [14: 16: 18] sts rem.
Cont straight until left front matches back to beg
of shoulder shaping, ending with RS facing for
next row.
Shape shoulder
Cast off 4 [5: 5: 6] sts at beg of next and foll alt
row.

Work 1 row.
Cast off rem 4 [4: 6: 6] sts.

RIGHT FRONT

Work to match left front, reversing shapings.

SLEEVES

Using smaller needles cast on 43 [45: 47: 47] sts.
Work in g st for 2 rows, ending with RS facing for
next row.
Change to larger needles.
Beg with a K row, work in st st, shaping sides by
inc 1 st at each end of 11th [9th: 9th: 7th] and
every foll 12th [10th: 10th: 8th] row to 59 [55:
67: 67] sts, then on every foll - [12th: -: 10th] row
until there are - [63: -: 71] sts.
Cont straight until sleeve meas 45 [46: 47: 47] cm,
ending with RS facing for next row.
Shape top
Cast off 6 [7: 8: 9] sts at beg of next 2 rows.
47 [49: 51: 53] sts.
Dec 1 st at each end of next 3 rows, then on foll
3 alt rows, then on every foll 4th row until 27 [29:
31: 33] sts rem.
Work 1 row.
Dec 1 st at each end of next and every foll alt row
to 19 sts, then on foll row, ending with RS facing
for next row.
Cast off rem 17 sts.

MAKING UP

Press as described on the information page.
Join both shoulder seams using back stitch, or
mattress stitch if preferred.
Front bands (both alike)
With RS facing and using smaller needles, pick
up and knit 60 [62: 64: 66] sts along front
opening edge, between cast-on edge and beg of
front slope shaping.
Work in g st for 2 rows, ending with **WS** facing for
next row.
Cast off knitwise (on **WS**).

Collar

Using smaller needles cast on 186 [190:
198: 202] sts.
Row 1 (RS): K2, *P2, K2, rep from * to end.
Row 2: P2, *K2, P2, rep from * to end.
These 2 rows form rib.
Keeping rib correct, cast off 3 sts at beg of next
48 [48: 50: 50] rows, ending with RS facing for
next row.
Cast off rem 42 [46: 48: 52] sts in rib.
Matching row-ends of collar to row-ends of front
bands, sew shaped cast-off edge of collar to
entire front and back neck edges.
See information page for finishing instructions,
setting in sleeves using the set-in method and
leaving an opening in right side seam 20 [21:
22: 23] cm up from cast-on edge. Cut ribbon into
2 equal lengths. Attach one end of each piece to
front opening edges level with opening in right
side seam.

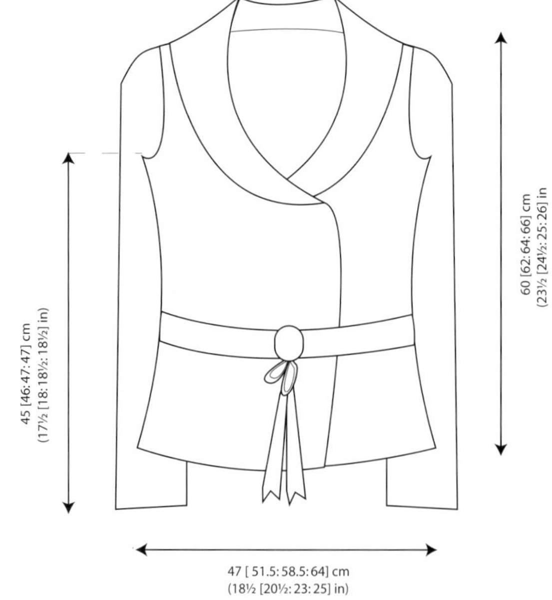

Main image page 33

Moira

YARN

	S	M	L	XL	
To fit bust	81-86	91-97	102-107	112-117	cm
	32-34	36-38	40-42	44-46	in

Rowan RYC Cashmere Tweed

	11	11	12	14	x 25gm

(photographed in Cambric 855)

Rowan RYC Wool Tweed

	6	6	6	7	x 50gm

NEEDLES

Cashmere Tweed version
1 pair 5mm (no 6) (US 8) needles
1 pair 6mm (no 4) (US 10) needles
5mm (no 6) (US 8) circular needle

Wool Tweed version
1 pair 4½mm (no 7) (US 7) needles
1 pair 5½mm (no 5) (US 9) needles
1 pair 4½mm (no 7) (US 7) circular needle

EXTRAS – 1 decorative kilt pin

TENSION

18 sts and 24 rows to 10 cm measured over
stocking stitch using larger needles.

BACK

Using larger needles cast on 73 [83: 93: 103] sts.
Beg with a K row, work in st st, shaping side
seams by inc 1 st at each end of 9th and every foll
8th row until there are 81 [91: 101: 111] sts.
Work 7 [9: 13: 15] rows, ending with RS facing for
next row.
Shape cap sleeves
Inc 1 st at each end of next and 3 foll alt rows,
then on foll 4 rows, ending with **WS** facing for
next row. 97 [107: 117: 127] sts.
Cont straight until armhole meas 23 [24: 25: 26] cm
from last increase, ending with RS facing for

next row.
Shape shoulders and back neck
Cast off 12 [13: 15: 16] sts at beg of next 2 rows.
73 [81: 87: 95] sts.
Next row (RS): Cast off 12 [13: 15: 16] sts, K until
there are 15 [18: 18: 21] sts on right needle and
turn, leaving rem sts on a holder.
Work each side of neck separately.
Cast off 4 sts at beg of next row.
Cast off rem 11 [14: 14: 17] sts.
With RS facing, rejoin yarn to rem sts, cast off
centre 19 [19: 21: 21] sts, K to end.
Complete to match first side, reversing shapings.

LEFT FRONT

Using larger needles cast on 2 sts.
Beg with a K row, work in st st as folls:
Work 1 row, ending with **WS** facing for next row.
Inc 1 st at beg (front opening edge) of next row
and at same edge on foll 15 [23: 29: 37] rows,
then on foll 11 [8: 7: 4] alt rows **and at same time**
inc 1 st at beg (side seam edge) of 8th and 3 foll
8th rows. 33 [38: 43: 48] sts.
Work 1 row, ending with RS facing for next row.
Shape cap sleeve
Inc 1 st at side seam edge of next and 3 foll alt
rows, then on foll 4 rows **and at same time** inc 1 st
at front opening edge of next and every foll alt
row. 47 [52: 57: 62] sts.
Inc 1 st at front opening edge **only** on 2nd and foll
alt row. 49 [54: 59: 64] sts.
Work 1 row, ending with RS facing for next row.
Shape front slope
Dec 1 st at end of next and foll 5 [4: 5: 4] alt rows,
then on every foll 4th row until 35 [40: 44: 49] sts
rem.
Cont straight until left front matches back to beg
of shoulder shaping, ending with RS facing for
next row.
Shape shoulder
Cast off 12 [13: 15: 16] sts at beg of next and foll

alt row.
Work 1 row.
Cast off rem 11 [14: 14: 17] sts.

RIGHT FRONT

Using larger needles cast on 2 sts.
Beg with a K row, work in st st as folls:
Work 1 row, ending with **WS** facing for next row.
Inc 1 st at end (front opening edge) of next row
and at same edge on foll 15 [23: 29: 37] rows,
then on foll 11 [8: 7: 4] alt rows **and at same time**
inc 1 st at end (side seam edge) of 8th and 3 foll
8th rows. 33 [38: 43: 48] sts.
Complete to match left front, reversing shapings.

MAKING UP

Press as described on the information page.
Join both shoulder seams using back stitch, or
mattress stitch if preferred.
Armhole borders (both alike)
With RS facing and using smaller needles, beg
and ending at last cap sleeve inc, pick up and knit
102 [106: 110: 114] sts along armhole row-end
edges.
Row 1 (WS): P2, *K2, P2, rep from * to end.
Row 2: K2, *P2, K2, rep from * to end.
These 2 rows form rib.
Work in rib for a further 4 rows, ending with **WS**
facing for next row.
Cast off in rib (on **WS**).
Join side and armhole border seams.
Hem border
With RS facing and using circular needle, beg and
ending at beg of front slope shaping, pick up and
knit 56 [59: 62: 65] sts down shaped left front
opening edge to base of left side seam, 74 [84:
94: 104] sts from back cast-on edge, then 56 [59:
62: 65] sts up shaped right front opening edge.
186 [202: 218: 234] sts.
Work in rib as given for armhole borders for 6 rows,
ending with **WS** facing for next row.

Cast off **loosely** in rib (on **WS**).

Collar

With RS facing and using circular needle, beg and
ending at cast-off edge of hem border, pick up
and knit 58 [60: 63: 65] sts up right front slope,
30 [30: 32: 32] sts from back, then 58 [60: 63: 65]
sts down left front slope.

146 [150: 158: 162] sts.

Work in rib as given for armhole borders for 19 cm.

Cast off in rib.

See information page for finishing instructions.
Fasten fronts with decorative kilt pin as in
photograph.

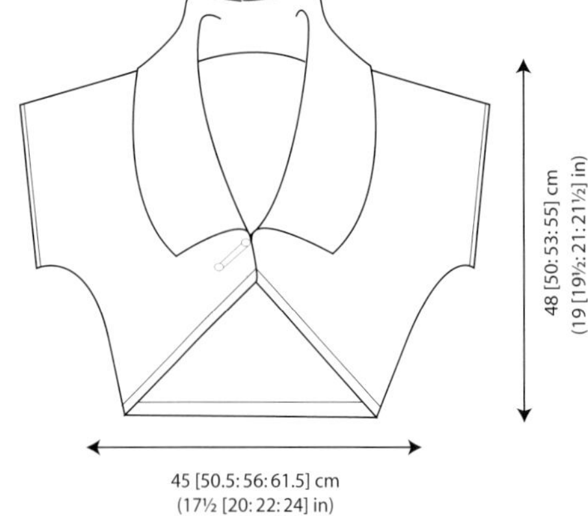

Main image page 10

Montrose

YARN

	S	M	L	XL	
To fit bust	81-86	91-97	102-107	112-117	cm
	32-34	36-38	40-42	44-46	in

Rowan RYC Cashmere Tweed

	46	49	54	58	x 25gm

Rowan RYC Wool Tweed

	23	25	27	29	x 50gm

(photographed in Reed 961)

NEEDLES

Cashmere Tweed version
1 pair 5mm (no 6) (US 8) needles
1 pair 6mm (no 4) (US 10) needles
5mm (no 6) (US 8) circular needle

Wool Tweed version
1 pair 4½mm (no 7) (US 7) needles
1 pair 5½mm (no 5) (US 9) needles
1 pair 4½mm (no 7) (US 7) circular needle

BUTTONS – 7 x 00410

TENSION

18 sts and 24 rows to 10 cm measured over
stocking stitch using larger needles.

BACK (worked from shoulder downwards)

Using 6mm (US 10) needles cast on 206 [218:
234: 244] sts.
Beg with a K row, work in st st until back meas
21 [22: 23: 24] cm, ending with RS facing for
next row.

Shape side edges
Dec 1 st at each end of next and 7 foll 4th rows,
then on foll 17 [17: 17: 19] alt rows, then on foll
23 [25: 27: 25] rows. 110 [118: 130: 140] sts.
Work 1 row, ending with **WS** facing for next row.
Next row (WS): P8 [1: 6: 6], P2tog, (P2 [3: 3: 3],

P2tog) 23 [23: 23: 25] times, P8 [0: 7: 7].
86 [94: 106: 114] sts.
Change to smaller needles.
Next row (RS): K2, *P2, K2, rep from * to end.
Next row: P2, *K2, P2, rep from * to end.
These 2 rows form rib.
Work in rib for a further 38 rows, ending with RS
facing for next row.
Cast off in rib.

LEFT FRONT (worked from shoulder downwards)

Using larger needles cast on 89 [95: 102: 107] sts.
Beg with a K row, work in st st for 4 rows, ending
with RS facing for next row.

Shape neck
Inc 1 st at beg of next and 2 foll 4th rows, then on
foll 2 [2: 3: 3] alt rows, then on foll 3 rows, ending
with RS facing for next row. 97 [103: 111: 116] sts.
Cast on 6 sts at beg of next row.
103 [109: 117: 122] sts.
Cont straight until left front meas 21 [22:
23: 24] cm, ending with RS facing for next row.

Shape side edge
Dec 1 st at end of next and 7 foll 4th rows, then
on foll 17 [17: 17: 19] alt rows, then on foll 23 [25:
27: 25] rows. 55 [59: 65: 70] sts.
Work 1 row, ending with **WS** facing for next row.
Next row (WS): P2 [4: 1: 1], P2tog, (P2 [2: 4: 4],
P2tog) 12 [12: 10: 11] times, P3 [5: 2: 1].
42 [46: 54: 58] sts.
Change to smaller needles.
Work in rib as given for back for 40 rows, ending
with RS facing for next row.
Cast off in rib.

RIGHT FRONT (worked from shoulder downwards)

Using larger needles cast on 89 [95: 102: 107] sts.
Beg with a K row, work in st st for 4 rows, ending
with RS facing for next row.

Shape neck
Inc 1 st at end of next and 2 foll 4th rows, then on

foll 2 [2: 3: 3] alt rows, then on foll 2 rows, ending
with **WS** facing for next row. 96 [102: 110: 115] sts.
Cast on 7 sts at beg of next row.
103 [109: 117: 122] sts.
Complete to match left front, reversing shapings.

MAKING UP

Press as described on the information page.
Join both shoulder/overarm seams using back
stitch, or mattress stitch if preferred.

Side edgings (both alike)
With RS facing and using circular needle, beg and
ending at top of rib, pick up and knit 206 [210:
214: 218] sts evenly along shaped and straight
row-end edges.
Work in g st for 2 rows, ending with **WS** facing for
next row.
Cast off knitwise (on **WS**).

Collar
With RS facing and using smaller needles, beg
and ending at front opening edges, pick up and
knit 27 [27: 28: 30] sts up right side of neck, 28 [28:
30: 30] sts from back, then 27 [27: 28: 30] sts down
left side of neck. 82 [82: 86: 90] sts.
Beg first row with P2, work in rib as given for
back for 13 cm.
Cast off in rib.

Collar bands (both alike)
With RS of collar (WS of body) facing and using
smaller needles, pick up and knit 28 sts along
row-end edge of collar, between cast-off edge
and pick-up row.
Row 1 (WS): K3, *P2, K2, rep from * to last st, K1.
Row 2: K1, P2, *K2, P2, rep from * to last st, K1.
These 2 rows form rib.
Work in rib for a further 8 rows, ending with **WS**
of collar facing for next row.
Cast off in rib (on **WS**).

Button band
With RS of body facing and using smaller
needles, pick up and knit 148 [152: 152: 156] sts

down left front opening edge, from collar pick-up
row to cast-off edge.
Work in rib as given for collar band for 10 rows,
ending with **WS** of band facing for next row.
Cast off in rib (on **WS**).

Buttonhole band
Work to match button band, picking up sts up
right front opening edge and with the addition of
7 buttonholes worked in row 6 as folls:
Row 6 (RS): Rib 4 [3: 3: 5], *cast off 2 sts (to
make a buttonhole – cast on 2 sts over these
cast-off sts on next row), rib until there are
21 [22: 22: 22] sts on right needle after cast-off,
rep from * 5 times more, cast off 2 sts (to make
7th buttonhole), rib to end.
Join row-end edges of front and back ribs and
side edgings to form side seams. Join ends of
collar bands to ends of front bands at neck edge.
See information page for finishing instructions.

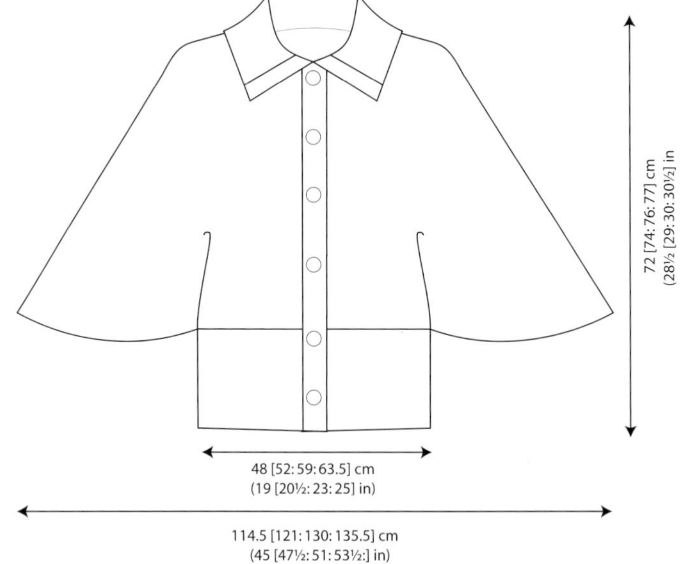

Main image page 31

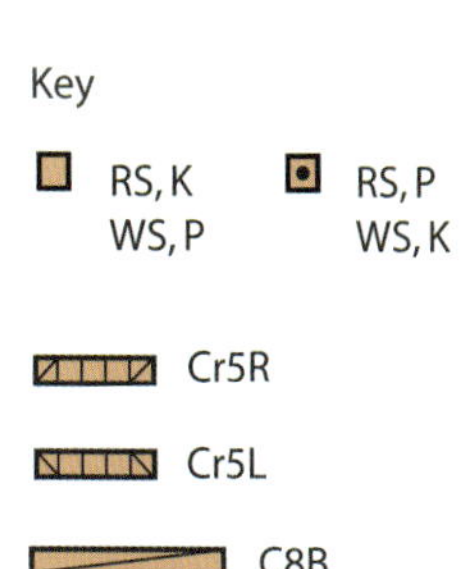 **Nessa**

YARN

	S	M	L	XL	
To fit bust	81-86	91-97	102-107	112-117	cm
	32-34	36-38	40-42	44-46	in

Rowan RYC Cashmere Tweed

	48	42	46	50	x 25gm

Rowan RYC Wool Tweed

	19	21	23	25	x 50gm

(photographed in Melton 960)

NEEDLES

Cashmere Tweed version
1 pair 5mm (no 6) (US 8) needles
1 pair 6mm (no 4) (US 10) needles
Cable needle

Wool Tweed version
1 pair 4½mm (no 7) (US 7) needles
1 pair 5½mm (no 5) (US 9) needles
Cable needle

TENSION

18 sts and 24 rows to 10 cm measured over
reverse stocking stitch using larger needles.

SPECIAL ABBREVIATIONS

Cr5R = slip next st onto cable needle and leave at
back of work, K4, then P1 from cable needle;
Cr5L = slip next 4 sts onto cable needle and leave
at front of work, P1, then K4 from cable needle;
C8B = slip next 4 sts onto cable needle and leave
at back of work, K4, then K4 from cable needle.

BACK

Using smaller needles cast on 86 [94: 106: 116] sts.
Row 1 (RS): K0 [0: 0: 1], P0 [0: 2: 2], *K2, P2, rep
from * to last 2 [2: 0: 1] sts, K2 [2: 0: 1].
Row 2: P0 [0: 0: 1], K0 [0: 2: 2], *P2, K2, rep from
* to last 2 [2: 0: 1] sts, P2 [2: 0: 1].
These 2 rows form rib.
Work in rib for a further 15 rows, ending with **WS**
facing for next row.
Row 18 (WS): Rib 36 [40: 46: 51], (M1, rib 2) twice,
(M1, rib 1) 3 times, (rib 1, M1) 3 times, (rib 2, M1)
twice, rib to end. 96 [104: 116: 126] sts.
Change to larger needles.

Cont in patt as folls:
Row 1 (RS): P36 [40: 46: 51], work next 24 sts as
row 1 of cable panel, P to end.
Row 2: K36 [40: 46: 51], work next 24 sts as row 2
of cable panel, K to end.
These 2 rows set the sts – centre cable panel with
rev st st at sides.
Cont as set until back meas 36 [37: 38: 39] cm,
ending with RS facing for next row.
Shape armholes
Keeping patt correct, cast off 5 [6: 7: 8] sts at beg
of next 2 rows. 86 [92: 102: 110] sts.
Dec 1 st at each end of next 3 [5: 7: 9] rows, then
on foll 3 [2: 2: 2] alt rows, then on foll 4th row.
72 [76: 82: 86] sts.
Cont straight until armhole meas 22 [23: 24: 25] cm,
ending with RS facing for next row.
Shape shoulders and back neck
Cast off 5 [6: 6: 7] sts at beg of next 2 rows.
62 [64: 70: 72] sts.
Next row (RS): Cast off 5 [6: 6: 7] sts, patt until
there are 9 [9: 11: 11] sts on right needle and turn,
leaving rem sts on a holder.

Work each side of neck separately.
Cast off 4 sts at beg of next row.
Cast off rem 5 [5: 7: 7] sts.
With RS facing, rejoin yarn to rem sts, cast off
centre 34 [34: 36: 36] sts, patt to end.
Complete to match first side, reversing shapings.

FRONT

Work as given for back until 16 [16: 18: 18] rows less
have been worked than on back to beg of shoulder
shaping, ending with RS facing for next row.
Shape neck
Next row (RS): Patt 22 [24: 27: 29] sts and turn,
leaving rem sts on a holder.
Work each side of neck separately.
Dec 1 st at neck edge of next 4 rows, then on foll
1 [1: 2: 2] alt rows, then on 2 foll 4th rows.
15 [17: 19: 21] sts.
Work 1 row, ending with RS facing for next row.
Shape shoulder
Cast off 5 [6: 6: 7] sts at beg of next and foll alt row.
Work 1 row.
Cast off rem 5 [5: 7: 7] sts.

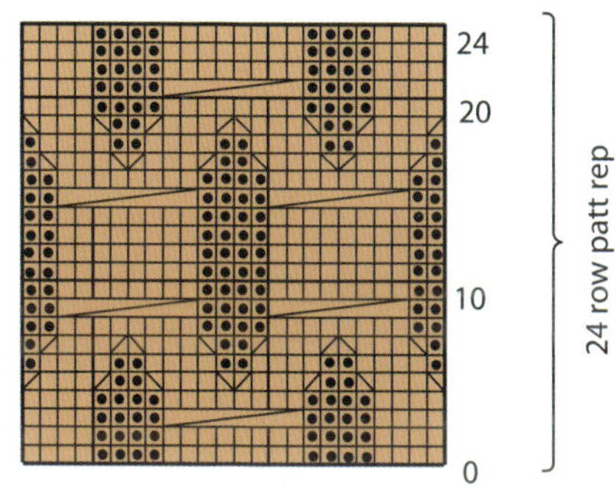

Key

	RS, K			RS, P
	WS, P			WS, K

Cr5R

Cr5L

C8B

With RS facing, rejoin yarn to rem sts, cast off
centre 28 sts, patt to end.
Complete to match first side, reversing shapings.

SLEEVES

Using smaller needles cast on 42 [44: 46: 46] sts.
Row 1 (RS): K0 [1: 0: 0], P2 [2: 0: 0], *K2, P2, rep
from * to last 0 [1: 2: 2] sts, K0 [1: 2: 2].
Row 2: P0 [1: 0: 0], K2 [2: 0: 0], *P2, K2, rep from
* to last 0 [1: 2: 2] sts, P0 [1: 2: 2].
These 2 rows form rib.
Work in rib for a further 15 rows, ending with **WS**
facing for next row.
Row 18 (WS): Rib 14 [15: 16: 16], (M1, rib 2) twice,
(M1, rib 1) 3 times, (rib 1, M1) 3 times, (rib 2, M1)
twice, rib to end. 52 [54: 56: 56] sts.
Change to larger needles.
Cont in patt as folls:
Row 1 (RS): P14 [15: 16: 16], work next 24 sts as
row 1 of cable panel, P to end.
Row 2: K14 [15: 16: 16], work next 24 sts as row 2
of cable panel, K to end.
These 2 rows set the sts – centre cable panel with
rev st st at sides.
Cont as set, shaping sides by inc 1 st at each end
of 5th [3rd: 3rd: 3rd] and every foll 8th [6th:
6th: 6th] row to 70 [58: 66: 82] sts, then on every
foll 10th [8th: 8th: 8th] row until there are 72 [76:
80: 84] sts, taking inc sts into rev st st.
Cont straight until sleeve meas 45 [46: 47: 47] cm,
ending with RS facing for next row.
Shape top
Keeping patt correct, cast off 5 [6: 7: 8] sts at beg
of next 2 rows. 62 [64: 66: 68] sts.
Dec 1 st at each end of next 3 rows, then on foll
3 alt rows, then on every foll 4th row until 44 [46:
48: 50] sts rem.
Work 1 row, ending with RS facing for next row.
Dec 1 st at each end of next and every foll alt row
to 34 sts, then on foll 5 rows, ending with RS
facing for next row.
Cast off rem 24 sts.

Press as described on the information page.
Join both shoulder seams using back stitch, or
mattress stitch if preferred.
Collar
Using smaller needles cast on 98 [98: 106: 106] sts.
Row 1 (RS): P0 [0: 2: 2], *K2, P2, rep from * to
last 2 [2: 0: 0] sts, K2 [2: 0: 0].
Row 2: K0 [0: 2: 2], *P2, K2, rep from * to last
2 [2: 0: 0] sts, P2 [2: 0: 0].
These 2 rows form rib.
Cont in rib until collar meas 9 cm, ending with RS
facing for next row.
Counting in from both ends of last row, place
markers after 25th [25th: 27th: 27th] st in from
each end of row (48 [48: 52: 52] sts between
markers).

Next row (RS): *Rib to within 1 st of marker, M1,
K2 (marker is between these 2 sts), M1, rep from
* once more, rib to end.
Next row: *Rib to within 1 st of marker, M1,
P2 (marker is between these 2 sts), M1, rep from
* once more, rib to end.
Rep last 2 rows 13 times more, then first of these 2
rows again, taking inc sts into rib and ending with
WS facing for next row. 214 [214: 222: 222] sts.
Work in rib across all sts for 2 rows, ending with
WS facing for next row.
Cast off in rib (on **WS**).
Join row-end edges of collar. Positioning markers
at centre front and centre back neck, sew cast-on
edge of collar to neck edge.
See information page for finishing instructions,
setting in sleeves using the set-in method.

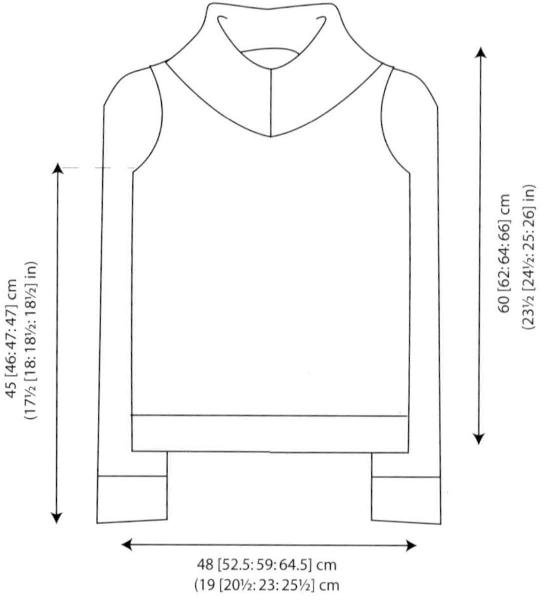

Main image page 24

Ross [ladies version]

YARN

	8	10	12	14	16	18	20	22	
To fit bust	81	86	91	97	102	107	112	117	cm
	32	34	36	38	40	42	44	46	in

Rowan RYC Cashmere Tweed

A

	15	15	15	16	17	18	18	19 x 25gm

B

	12	12	12	13	14	15	15	16 x 50gm

Rowan RYC Wool Tweed

A Mull 955

	7	7	8	8	9	9	9	10 x 50gm

B Reed 961

	6	6	6	7	7	7	7	8 x 50gm

NEEDLES

Cashmere Tweed version

1 pair 5mm (no 6) (US 8) needles
1 pair 6mm (no 4) (US 10) needles
5mm (no 6) (US 8) circular needle

Wool Tweed version

1 pair 4½mm (no 7) (US 7) needles
1 pair 5½mm (no 5) (US 9) needles
1 pair 4½mm (no 7) (US 7) circular needle

TENSION

18 sts and 24 rows to 10 cm measured over stocking stitch using larger needles.

BACK

Using smaller needles and yarn A cast on
78 [82: 86: 90: 98: 102: 110: 114] sts.
Row 1 (RS): K2, *P2, K2, rep from * to end.
Row 2: P2, *K2, P2, rep from * to end.
These 2 rows form rib.
Work in rib for a further 16 rows, inc [inc: inc: inc: dec: inc: dec: dec] 1 st at end of last row and ending with RS facing for next row.
79 [83: 87: 91: 97: 103: 109: 113] sts.
Change to larger needles.
Join in yarn B and, beg with a K row, work in striped st st as folls:
Using yarn B, work 8 rows.

Using yarn A, work 8 rows, dec 1 st at each end of first and 7th of these rows and ending with RS facing for next row.
75 [79: 83: 87: 93: 99: 105: 109] sts.
These 16 rows form striped st st and beg side seam shaping.
Cont in striped st st, shaping side seams by dec 1 st at each end of 5th and foll 4th row.
71 [75: 79: 83: 89: 95: 101: 105] sts.
Work 9 rows, ending with RS facing for next row.
Inc 1 st at each end of next and every foll 6th row until there are 79 [83: 87: 91: 97: 103: 109: 113] sts.
Cont straight until back meas approx 32 [32: 31: 34: 33: 35: 34: 36] cm, ending after 6 [6: 4: 4: 8: 6: 4: 8] rows using yarn A [A: A: B: A: B: B: B] and with RS facing for next row.
Shape raglan armholes
Keeping stripes correct, cast off 2 sts at beg of next 2 rows. 75 [79: 83: 87: 93: 99: 105: 109] sts.
Dec 1 st at each end of next 1 [1: 3: 7: 9: 15: 19: 23] rows, then on 2 [0: 0: 0: 0: 0: 0: 0] foll 4th rows, then on every foll alt row until 25 [25: 25: 25: 27: 27: 27: 27] sts rem.
Work 1 row, ending with RS facing for next row.
Cast off.

FRONT

Work as given for back to beg of raglan armhole shaping, ending with RS facing for next row.
Shape raglan and divide for neck
Next row (RS): Cast off 2 sts, K until there are 37 [39: 41: 43: 46: 49: 52: 54] sts on right needle and turn, leaving rem sts on a holder.
Work each side of neck separately.
Keeping stripes correct, work 1 row.
Dec 1 st at raglan armhole edge of next 1 [1: 3: 7: 9: 15: 19: 23] rows, then on 2 [0: 0: 0: 0: 0: 0: 0] foll 4th rows, then on foll 20 [24: 24: 22: 22: 19: 18: 16] alt rows **and at same time** dec 1 st at neck edge of 3rd and 11 [11: 11: 11: 12: 12: 12: 12] foll 4th rows. 2 sts.
Work 1 row, ending with RS facing for next row.
Next row (RS): K2tog and fasten off.
With RS facing, slip centre st onto a holder, K to end.

Complete to match first side, reversing shapings.

SLEEVES

Using smaller needles and yarn A cast on
42 [42: 46: 46: 46: 46: 50: 50] sts.
Work in rib as given for back for 18 rows, inc [inc: dec: dec: inc: inc: dec: dec] 1 st at end of last row and ending with RS facing for next row.
43 [43: 45: 45: 47: 47: 49: 49] sts.
Change to 6mm (US 10) needles.
Join in yarn B.
Beg with a K row and 6 [6: 2: 2: 8: 2: 2: 6] rows using yarn B [B: A: B: B: B: B: A], work in striped st st as given for back, shaping sides by inc 1 st at each end of 5th and every foll 6th row to 59 [59: 59: 59: 59: 59: 63: 63] sts, then on every foll 8th row until there are 67 [67: 69: 69: 71: 71: 73: 73] sts.
Cont straight until sleeve meas approx 44 [44: 45: 45: 46: 46: 45: 45] cm, ending after same stripe row as on back to beg of raglan armhole shaping and with RS facing for next row.
Shape raglan
Keeping stripes correct, cast off 2 sts at beg of next 2 rows. 63 [63: 65: 65: 67: 67: 69: 69] sts.
Dec 1 st at each end of next and every foll alt row until 13 sts rem.
Work 1 row, ending with RS facing for next row.
Left sleeve only
Dec 1 st at each end of next row, then cast off 4 sts at beg of foll row. 7 sts.
Dec 1 st at beg of next row, then cast off 3 sts at beg of foll row.
Right sleeve only
Cast off 5 sts at beg and dec 1 st at end of next row. 7 sts.
Work 1 row.
Cast off 3 sts at beg and dec 1 st at end of next row.
Work 1 row.
Both sleeves
Cast off rem 3 sts.

MAKING UP

Press as described on the information page.
Join both front and both back raglan armhole

seams using back stitch, or mattress stitch if preferred.

Neckband

With RS facing, using circular needle and yarn A, beg and ending at left back raglan seam, pick up and knit 9 sts from left sleeve,

51 [51: 51: 51: 55: 55: 55: 55] sts down left side of neck, K st from holder at base of V and mark this st with a coloured thread, pick up and knit 51 [51: 51: 51: 55: 55: 55: 55] sts up right side of neck, 9 sts from right sleeve, then 26 sts from back.

147 [147: 147: 147: 155: 155: 155: 155] sts.

Round 1 (RS): *K2, P2, rep from * to within 4 sts of marked st, K2, K2tog tbl, K marked st, K2tog, **K2, P2, rep from ** to end.

This round sets position of rib.

Keeping rib correct, cont as folls:

Round 2: Rib to within 2 sts of marked st, K2tog tbl, K marked st, K2tog, rib to end.

Rep last round 6 times more.

131 [131: 131: 131: 139: 139: 139: 139] sts.
Cast off in rib, still decreasing either side of marked st as before.

See information page for finishing instructions.

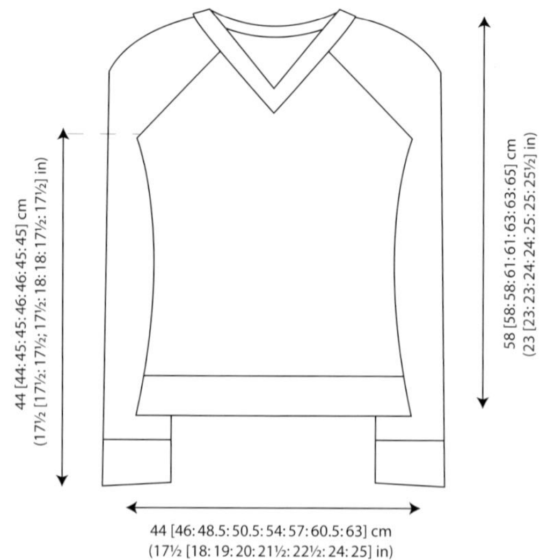

Main image page 16

YARN

	S	M	L	XL	XXL	
To fit chest	102	107	112	117	122	cm
	40	42	44	46	48	in

Rowan RYC Cashmere Tweed

A	22	22	23	25	26	x 25gm
B	17	18	19	20	21	x 50gm

Rowan RYC Wool Tweed

A Shetland 953	11	11	12	12	13	x 50gm
B Ottoman 959	9	9	9	10	10	x 50gm

NEEDLES

Cashmere Tweed version
1 pair 5mm (no 6) (US 8) needles
1 pair 6mm (no 4) (US 10) needles
5mm (no 6) (US 8) circular needle

Wool Tweed version
1 pair 4½mm (no 7) (US 7) needles
1 pair 5½mm (no 5) (US 9) needles
1 pair 4½mm (no 7) (US 7) circular needle

TENSION

18 sts and 24 rows to 10 cm measured over
stocking stitch using larger needles.

BACK

Using smaller needles and yarn A cast on
106 [110: 114: 122: 126] sts.
Row 1 (RS): K2, *P2, K2, rep from * to end.
Row 2: P2, *K2, P2, rep from * to end.
These 2 rows form rib.
Work in rib for a further 16 rows, dec [inc: inc:
dec: inc] 1 st at end of last row and ending with
RS facing for next row. 105 [111: 115: 121: 127] sts.
Change to larger needles.
Join in yarn B and, beg with a K row, work in
striped st st as folls:
Using yarn B, work 8 rows.

Using yarn A, work 8 rows.
These 16 rows form striped st st.
Cont in striped st st until back meas approx
37 [38: 37: 38: 37] cm, ending after 2 [4: 2: 4: 2]
rows using yarn A and with RS facing for next row.
Shape raglan armholes
Keeping stripes correct, cast off 6 sts at beg of
next 2 rows. 93 [99: 103: 109: 115] sts.
Dec 1 st at each end of next 1 [5: 5: 9: 11] rows,
then on every foll alt row until 27 [27: 29:
29: 31] sts rem.
Work 1 row, ending with RS facing for next row.
Cast off.

FRONT

Work as given for back until 75 [77: 81: 83: 87] sts
rem in raglan armhole shaping.
Work 1 row, ending with RS facing for next row.
Shape raglan and divide for neck
Next row (RS): K2tog, K35 [36: 38: 39: 41] and
turn, leaving rem sts on a holder.
Work each side of neck separately.
Keeping stripes correct, work 1 row.
Dec 1 st at raglan armhole edge of next and foll
20 [21: 22: 23: 24] alt rows **and at same time** dec
1 st at neck edge of next and foll 5 [4: 5: 4: 5] alt
rows, then on 7 [8: 8: 9: 9] foll 4th rows. 2 sts.
Work 1 row, ending with RS facing for next row.
Next row (RS): K2tog and fasten off.
With RS facing, slip centre st onto a holder, K to
last 2 sts, K2tog.
Complete to match first side, reversing shapings.

SLEEVES

Using smaller needles and yarn A cast on
46 [46: 50: 50: 54] sts.
Work in rib as given for back for 18 rows, dec [inc:
dec: inc: dec] 1 st at end of last row and ending
with RS facing for next row. 45 [47: 49: 51: 53] sts.
Change to larger needles.
Join in yarn B.

Beg with a K row and 8 [2: 2: 4: 2] rows using
yarn B [A: B: B: A], work in striped st st as given
for back, shaping sides by inc 1 st at each end of
3rd and every foll 4th [4th: 4th: 4th: 6th] row to
65 [63: 59: 57: 91] sts, then on every foll 6th [6th:
6th: 6th: -] row until there are 83 [85: 87: 89: -] sts.
Cont straight until sleeve meas approx 50 [52: 54:
56: 58] cm, ending after same stripe row as on
back to beg of raglan armhole shaping and with
RS facing for next row.
Shape raglan
Keeping stripes correct, cast off 6 sts at beg of
next 2 rows. 71 [73: 75: 77: 79] sts.
Dec 1 st at each end of next and every foll alt row
until 9 sts rem.
Work 1 row, ending with RS facing for next row.
Left sleeve only
Dec 1 st at each end of next row, then cast off 2 sts
at beg of foll row. 5 sts.
Dec 1 st at beg of next row, then cast off 2 sts at
beg of foll row.
Right sleeve only
Cast off 3 sts at beg and dec 1 st at end of next
row. 5 sts.
Work 1 row.
Cast off 2 sts at beg and dec 1 st at end of next
row.
Work 1 row.
Both sleeves
Cast off rem 2 sts.

MAKING UP

Press as described on the information page.
Join both front and both back raglan armhole
seams using back stitch, or mattress stitch if
preferred.
Neckband
With RS facing, using circular needle and yarn A,
beg and ending at left back raglan seam, pick up
and knit 8 sts from left sleeve, 44 [48: 48:
52: 52] sts down left side of neck, K st from

holder at base of V and mark this st with a
coloured thread, pick up and knit 44 [48: 48:
52: 52] sts up right side of neck, 8 sts from right
sleeve, then 26 [26: 30: 30: 30] sts from back.
131 [139: 143: 151: 151] sts.
Round 1 (RS): *K2, P2, rep from * to within 4 sts
of marked st, K2, K2tog tbl, K marked st, K2tog,
**K2, P2, rep from ** to end.
This round sets position of rib.
Keeping rib correct, cont as folls:
Round 2: Rib to within 2 sts of marked st, K2tog
tbl, K marked st, K2tog, rib to end.
Rep last round 6 times more.
115 [123: 127: 135: 135] sts.
Cast off in rib, still decreasing either side of
marked st as before.
See information page for finishing instructions.

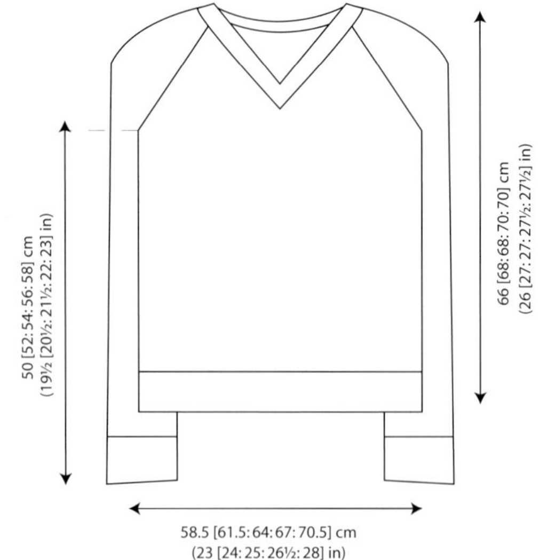

- Our sizing now conforms to standard clothing sizes. Therefore if you buy a standard size 12 in clothing, then our size 12 or Medium patterns will fit you perfectly.

- Dimensions in the charts below are body measurements, not garment dimensions, therefore please refer to the measuring guide to help you to determine which is the best size for you to knit.

STANDARD SIZING GUIDE FOR WOMEN

UK SIZE	8	10	12	14	16	18	20	22	
USA Size	6	8	10	12	14	16	18	20	
EUR Size	34	36	38	40	42	44	46	48	
To fit bust	32	34	36	38	40	42	44	46	inches
	82	87	92	97	102	107	112	117	cm
To fit waist	24	26	28	30	32	34	36	38	inches
	61	66	71	76	81	86	91	96	cm
To fit hips	34	6	38	40	42	44	46	48	inches
	87	92	97	102	107	112	117	122	cm

CASUAL SIZING GUIDE FOR WOMEN

As there are some designs that are intended to fit more generously, we have introduced our casual sizing guide. The designs that fall into this group can be recognised by the size range: Small, Medium, Large & Xlarge. Each of these sizes cover two sizes from the standard sizing guide, ie. Size S will fit sizes 8/10, size M will fit sizes 12/14 and so on. The sizing within this chart is also based on the larger size within the range, ie. M will be based on size 14.

UK SIZE	S	M	L	XL	
DUAL SIZE	8/10	12/14	16/18	20/22	
To fit bust	32 – 34	36 – 38	40 – 42	44 – 46	inches
	82 – 87	92 - 97	102 – 107	112 – 117	cm
To fit waist	24 – 26	28 – 30	32 – 34	36 – 38	inches
	61 – 66	71 – 76	81 – 86	91 – 96	cm
To fit hips	34 – 36	38 – 40	42 – 44	46 – 48	inches
	87 – 92	97 – 102	107 – 112	117 – 122	cm

STANDARD SIZING GUIDE FOR MEN

UK SIZE	S	M	L	XL	XXL	
EUR Size	50	52	54	56	58	
To fit chest	40	42	44	46	48	inches
	102	107	112	117	122	cm
To fit waist	32	34	36	38	40	inches
	81	86	91	96	101	cm

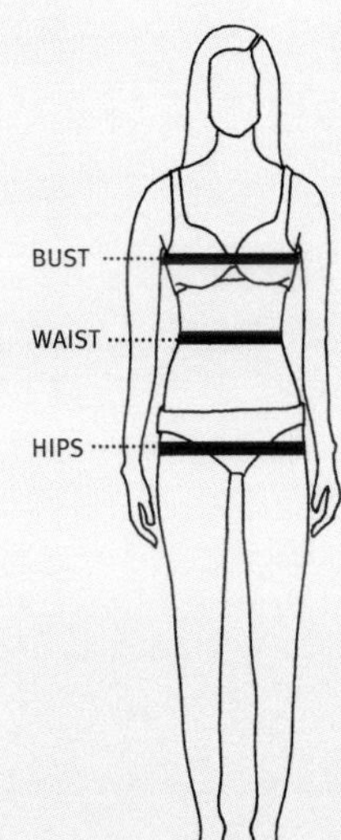

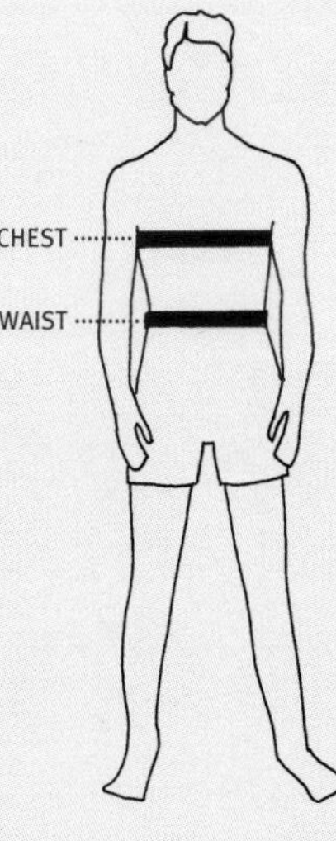

MEASURING GUIDE

For maximum comfort and to ensure the correct fit when choosing a size to knit, please follow the tips below when checking your size.

Measure yourself close to your body, over your underwear and don't pull the tape measure too tight!

Bust/chest – measure around the fullest part of the bust/chest and across the shoulder blades.

Waist – measure around the natural waistline, just above the hip bone.

Hips – measure around the fullest part of the bottom.

If you don't wish to measure yourself, note the size of a favourite jumper that you like the fit of. Our sizes are now comparable to the clothing sizes from the major high street retailers, so if your favourite jumper is a size Medium or size 12, then our casual size Medium and standard size 12 should be approximately the same fit.

To be extra sure, measure your favourite jumper and then compare these measurements with the size diagram given at the end of the individual instructions.

Finally, once you have decided which size is best for you, please ensure that you achieve the tension required for the design you wish to knit. Remember if your tension is too loose, your garment will be bigger than the pattern size and you may use more yarn. If your tension is too tight, your garment could be smaller than the pattern size and you will have yarn left over. Furthermore if your tension is incorrect, the handle of your fabric will be too stiff or floppy and will not fit properly. It really does make sense to check your tension before starting every project.